Chocolate Kisses

Chocolate Kisses

Ann Wade

Ivy House
Publishing Group
www.ivyhousebooks.com

PUBLISHED BY IVY HOUSE PUBLISHING GROUP
5122 Bur Oak Circle, Raleigh, NC 27612
United States of America
919-782-0281
www.ivyhousebooks.com

ISBN: 1-57197-458-X
Library of Congress Control Number: 2005909044

Printed in the United States of America

For my friends
Past - Present - Future

Contents

Blessed are they who have the gift of making friends, for it is one of God's best gifts. It involves many things, but above all, the power of going out of one's self, and appreciating whatever is noble and loving in another.

—THOMAS HUGHES

Prologue

When do we claim another as a friend? We often prize similar viewpoints and tastes; frequent time together; sharing deepest emotions, spoken or unspoken; presence awaiting presence.

What are the criteria on which we judge a friend as a friend? Yes, we value loyalty through thick and thin; forgiveness for slights and absences; generosity in gifts, times, words, empathy; constancy in being faithful and steadfast and possibly many other traits that emanate from our diversity.

How often do we take friends for granted? We expect the skills of mind reading, the ability to overlook wrongs and deficiencies, and the charity to accept one another without definition.

Why do we need friends? We find it just plain lonely without them. Relationships offer our biggest opportunity for learning and personal growth. We can learn both what we are meant to be and what we don't want to be.

Friendships thrive on nourishment and the depth of friendships depends on the quantity and quality of nourishment received. When friends connect and identify at the deepest levels of self, they are often called soul mates; they are one, a wholeness that does not dissolve.

This story is a witness of friends serving friends, of ordinary people doing extraordinary things for another, a model of friendship as one of God's gifts. Friends are not saints, people without faults; they just behave as saints when they serve to the highest calling of friendship.

My thanks to the many friends of Sandy Weisenburger, who were instrumental in making this memoir of her possible.

Stan Kolden, both Sandy's neighbor and friend for twenty-five years, ever dependable and present in caring for her welfare and keeping her friends informed; his e-mails and telephone calls were excellent references for the unfolding of this story.

Glyn Northington, as a friend of Stan's, he became a friend of Sandy's. His anecdotes helped to relate the humorous aspects of Sandy's personality.

Barb Bakken, who was the crucial contact and advocate for Sandy between doctors and hospitals; her e-mails and telephone calls were full of the details of the medical challenges that confronted Sandy.

Her nephew, Larry Sanderson, and nieces, Myra Weisenburger and Karen Erickson, who from their devotion shared their family times and their love for their Aunt Sandy.

Mary Bruun and Patty LaBerge, whose friendship with Sandy stretched back the longest in years and provided personal stories that were invaluable.

Jan Hackley and Marilyn Berdahl, whose long-time association with Sandy began within the business arena, and their delight in knowing her enhanced this story of friendship.

Mary Ann Mead, Gert Wehking, Louiva Puffer, and Carol Joyce, her pastor, whose friendships originated from membership in a church that was a true home for Sandy's beliefs.

Peggy Leppik who added a political perspective to Sandy's party preference and commitments. And thanks to Congressman Jim Ramstad who sent his personal words of appreciation to Sandy.

Vicki Nicole and Amy Hodgson, whose friendship came in the last months of Sandy's life. Without a long history with her, they spoke to Sandy's character with fresh impressions.

Patsy Vessey, my long-time friend, who became a friend of Sandy's through our social activities of the '90s. She was with her when I couldn't.

Surely, there are many more friends, who while unknown to me were caring and present with Sandy. To all friends and friendships, I dedicate this story and thank you for the richness that you add to the meaning of life.

Thanks to readers Rose Meer, Mary Nelson, Valerie DelCurto, and Robert Zoller, who read my first draft and encouraged me to go all the way. Their feedback spurred me on.

I extend appreciation to new friends and writers, Laurie Klemme and Cyndi Coyne, who helped with story structure and editing. Their suggestions, persuasion, and ideas were the challenges I needed to develop the subtleties in the story. They helped me become a better writer, and I am thankful to them for that.

My gratitude to the Executive Director of The ALS Association, Minnesota Chapter, Susan Spalding who is an impressive young woman and gave unconditional support to Sandy and my story.

And, a final acknowledgment to Ivy House Publishing Group, who showed their confidence in me by accepting my second book, *Chocolate Kisses*, for publication. It is a pleasure to work with the Ivy House staff.

My Friend, Sandy

Ann

It was a fall day in 1979 when I picked up the phone to hear an unfamiliar voice. I'd been in Minneapolis two months, recently relocated from Arizona.

"Hello Ann, I understand you've just moved to Minneapolis."

Oh, no, a telemarketer, I thought, as I said a slow "Yes."

"I'm Sandy Weisenburger and we have a mutual friend in Tucson, Sally Prichert. I saw her recently at a convention and she told me of your move. She suggested I call you . . . thought you might need a friend in your new city."

Wow, that's quite a reach. I knew Sally as an occasional substitute in my Tucson bridge club, which had disbanded at least eight years ago. She must have heard of my move from mutual friends. What a coincidence or act of providence for Sandy and Sally to talk about me.

I knew that people are often asked by acquaintances to cold call someone in their locality, but this was the first time to experience someone actually following through. Later I would discover that not extending a personal welcome to a stranger would have denied the essence of Sandy's personality. Her cherubic appearance was the right persona for her warm, thoughtful manner.

"How about meeting for dinner?"

"Yes, let's do. I'm not real familiar with the city yet nor have I had the chance to meet many people."

"Well, maybe I can help with both. How about Tuesday at Pauline's on 394 which is easy to get to off of 169."

"Yes, I can find that."

"I'll wait for you in the foyer and wear a lavender scarf, my favorite color. Shall we say six o'clock?"

"I look forward to meeting you." I answered full of expectancy to know this friendly voice. My mind started a search for an article of lavender to wear also.

If loyalty, steadfastness, and generosity are traits you value in a friend, Sandy would be your woman. If looking for someone to organize a project, chair a fundraiser, or build community, Sandy would be your woman. Friends were abundant in her life. She honored them with personal attention; they were not just ships passing in the night, rather they became like prized possessions. She was always there for others and now came a difficult time when her dearest friends would be there for her. When dying, you need others to survive.

Amyotrophic Lateral Sclerosis (ALS, Lou Gehrig's disease) is neither a friendly nor a dignified disease; it's frightening, lonely, and depressing. It renders one powerless. One becomes totally dependent upon others; there are no options. Those many friendships nurtured by Sandy translated into her blessings, and I suspect humility for the rest of us, as we faced her toughest challenge.

As Sandy and I talked over dinner, we found common ground and began our friendship. We were of the same age, forty-nine, which I had to deduce over time. It was only after many birthday celebrations that I surmised we were both born in 1930, which was later confirmed by the host of her surprise 70th birthday party. Even though she was social and gregarious and voiced strong viewpoints, she had personal items that she kept private. Two of those secrets were her birth year and given name. She wanted us to believe that she was born as Sandy.

We were also both divorced but with different residual feelings; she had no time or kind words for men in general. As for me, I was still seeking a male companion. We both had responsible positions in large corporations having worked ourselves up the ladder. We both liked the theater; although I could forego a Shakespeare play, she could not. Guess what—she artfully cajoled me to see every Shakespeare production at the Guthrie Theater. We loved pets, though of different types. Cats were Sandy's children and there was no love left for dogs, which were my preferred pets. We both played bridge, I more avidly and recently than she, but she yielded over time to a once-a-month dinner and game with my bridge-playing friends.

Sandy had the prettiness of a joyful, innocent, untainted child. Her soft brown curly hair, always short, was like a cap of cashmere. She was my height, maybe five-four; her figure rounded and attractively attired often in soft fabrics of her favorite pale shades of lavender, greens and beige set-off with colorful scarves. Her appearance, energies and greetings were warm and kindly, but underneath was a headstrong, long-lasting determination that aided her in all of her chosen endeavors.

Through knowing her, I became aware that I tended to revolve in and out of friendships, more random with invitations, outings, and coffee or cocktail chats—maybe because I'd lived in four different cities and had to leave friends behind too often. I saw that Sandy was more constant in keeping one-on-one contact with others: neighbors in for weekend brunch, holiday parties for business associates, social gatherings for strangers to make acquaintance, and soliciting persons for community projects. I admired her trait of constancy and maybe even envied the broad social life that resulted. Never once was I with her in public that she wasn't recognized and greeted by at least a half-dozen persons. Maybe that is the blessing of having lived in one city for your adult life and having the attributes to earn the respect that was shown to her.

My high regard for her work in building community knew no bounds. Sandy was an organizer and an achiever, she wanted things to happen for people and she strived for faultless results. She seldom said no to a request for her assistance; hence, her name was at the top of many lists as a responsible person who could be trusted to carry the ball all the way. She was the spearhead and prime mover of many causes. Her rosy, chubby cheeks and soft brown doe-like eyes disguised her other side, the stern taskmaster with herself and others. She never backed away from a challenge, and she made a difference in a variety of ways. I can speak of the few I knew about.

Sandy was a long-time employee of General Mills—thirty-five years. Whenever I met a General Mills employee within my business circles, during the '80s and '90s when I worked in Minneapolis, I found they knew Sandy and her reputation for getting things done. Even with retirement, she never really left General Mills. The company approached her to be Director of Programs for Retired Volunteers, and she was instrumental in keeping 250 volunteers connected to community needs for five years. Only ALS halted her work.

In 1991, the Governor of Minnesota appointed Sandy to head a State Advisory Committee to organize a Board Office of Citizenship and Volunteer Services. The

Committee met three times a year and served as an umbrella office for all volunteer services and programs in the state; they became a source of education and resources for Directors of volunteer programs. Under her leadership the Office published a newsletter, conducted workshops, and provided consulting services. To her disappointment, the group was disbanded eight years later by a then newly elected governor. She chalked it up as a decision made by a dumb male politician.

Above all, Sandy was an adamant backer of the Republican Party and promoted their candidates and policies formally and informally. In 1980, Sandy became the Chair of Minnesota Senate District 45, the organization working for the election of the State Senator from the Plymouth area of suburban Minneapolis. Jim Ramstad would be campaigning for his first term, and Sandy recruited support for Jim, both in people and dollars. Jim won his first campaign as well as every one thereafter. Jim was elected to Congress in 1990 where he still serves the people of the western suburban area of the Twin Cities. His handwritten note sent to Sandy a few months after her diagnosis expresses how he valued her work and friendship.

> *Our good friend, Barb, told me of your illness, and I want you to know you're in my thoughts and prayers. I will* always *be grateful to you, dear friend, for your key support and important volunteer work on my very first campaign (1980). Without your help then, I would not be in Congress today. I miss you and hope you're feeling better, Sandy. God bless, and call if I can be helpful.*
> *Your friend always,*
> *Jim Ramstad*

Sandy was well versed in the Minnesota political processes and this led her to help revitalize the Suburban Republican Women Chapter in Minneapolis. It was a struggling organization when she stepped into its leadership position early in the '90s. She enlisted friends for membership, handing out flyers, and hosting neighborhood gatherings. She wanted us to be politically astute and raise funds for female candidates. I was one of the many she recruited. She had convincing answers for questions such as: "Exactly what is the party's policy?" "How should I vote, Sandy?" or "Tell me about the candidates" or "What do I do in a caucus?" or "Who should I back?" Sandy's persuasive powers seldom failed. I marveled how I so easily signed on to her pleas for time and contributions. She was not above laying a light coating of guilt; her words were so full of expectation that you couldn't say no to her worthy causes. She could be dictatorial when her belief and commitment were strong—arguing with her was to no avail. I believe she was disappointed her co-members did not dedicate themselves to the same degree as she. The chapter eventually melded in with another chapter where she was not as active.

Her visibility in the local Party prompted a request from a new political candidate, Peggy Leppik who was to run for State Representative. Sandy was Chair for all of Peggy's campaigns, and Peggy was successfully elected for six terms (two years each term). Peggy visited Sandy every week during her illness and personally told me: "I would never had become a representative without Sandy. Her leadership was awesome for which I am ever grateful."

It's interesting to note that Sandy died on the first Tuesday of November, Election Day.

Sandy brought professional women together when she organized the Minneapolis Chapter of Epsilon Sigma Alpha. It was a gathering of her many friends, which blossomed into a broad network across diverse business careers. Most of us became volunteers in each other's favorite charities or projects and mentors to others when needed. Sandy's leadership was invaluable as she served in the positions of Chapter President, State Vice President and then President, and a member of the International Board. She was instrumental in starting other chapters and volunteered many hours in coaching their new officers.

Her last endeavor seemed to please her the most. Through a friend from General Mills, Sandy became acquainted with the United Church of Christ. The two attended a travelogue on Israel one evening and a Sunday service the following week. The diversity she saw in the congregation appealed to her. All persons, races, cultures, genders were welcomed; the Church's inclusive message matched hers. As typical of Sandy, who was not one to sit on the sidelines, she became an active member.

She was elected twice by the congregation to be Moderator, the top elected official and the church's delegate to state conferences. This in essence is acting as president of the church and fulfilling the duties of chairperson for the Executive Council meetings. The United Church of Christ is very liberal in perspective and Sandy, while open minded, was a staunch Republican. She learned to stand aside when she found it ill advised to oppose church members just because they were Democrats.

Sandy also served two years as Chair of the Stewardship Committee, whose work was to gather monetary pledges sufficient for the upcoming annual budget. She met a last time with this Committee, hosting a morning coffee in her home several weeks before she moved to an assisted-living apartment at Jones-Harrison Home. It was December 2002 and, although just three months after diagnosis, Sandy no longer had use of her legs.

It's painful to watch the end of a productive life. Her body shut down, progressing from her feet upwards; only fourteen months from diagnosis to her last breath. During that time with its short horizon, I witnessed yet again her manner of generosity, hospitality, and kindness to everyone who entered her room—friends and caregivers alike. She maintained her dignity even in the face of the indignities of ALS. I watched how modesty and privacy has to be set aside when one's body is harnessed for lifting from chair to bathroom to bed and personal functions tended to by male aides. Sandy attempted to lighten her sensitivity and their embarrassment with bits of humor, questions about their families, and always a "thank you for helping me." She detested being a burden upon anyone else and now she had to be exactly that.

It was May 2003 when I made my first visit to her at Jones-Harrison. Her face lit up with a smile as I entered her room on the third floor. It was vintage Sandy, her smiling doll-like face, brown and curly hair cropped short framing a high forehead, finely trimmed eyebrows arched above deep-set twinkling brown eyes, and soft rosy cherub cheeks showing few lines of her seventy-two years. She was dressed with flair in a black knit dress, silver jewelry on her bosom, fingers and ears and both face and nails prettily made up. The noticeable difference was the motorized wheel chair in which she sat, immobile from the waist down and the droop of her head slouched to the left side. She'd always had a personal habit of tilting her head to the left, a characteristic now permanent. I pressed a kiss on her forehead as she squeezed my hand.

The room was bright and cheery. A large window stretched along the outside wall, and furniture from her home—desk, dressers, pictures, chairs, and lamps—made it Sandy's place. The deep windowsill was dressed with flowers from end to end. Vases of lavender gladioli from one friend's garden and colorful mixed bouquets from others were interspersed with green plants. It was like a border between an inside and outside world.

Visits with Sandy were filled with reminiscence, tears, laughter, hard facts about ALS, clinic visits, and shopping lists. I hadn't seen her since my move to Iowa two years previously, but as true friendship proves out, remoteness and absence do not dim affection and straight talk. Bits of our conversations were like:

"Sandy, can we talk about the tough stuff?"

"Maybe, but if we start crying we have to stop."

and another,

"Since I volunteer at the University hospital, I accessed their computer library to learn about ALS. I found lots of technical information but it didn't answer my question of how fast it progresses."

"Well, the doctors say it's different for each individual. The rate of progress remains the same throughout . . . like if it begins slow, then it's slow all the way." She paused. "Don't think it's going to take too long, Ann. Mine seems to be moving quickly, so I assume it will probably stay that way."

There was no response I could make to take that thought away.

Later, I asked, "Are you afraid, Sandy?"

"Mostly of choking or suffocating. The doctors said

they'd make me comfortable and not let that happen. But, I'm not sure I trust them on that yet." We sat quiet for a moment before she said, "I'd rather starve than suffocate, but they told me starving to death was much more painful than I realize."

I knew I was nearing her boundaries when I asked: "Sandy, how do you handle this emotionally?" She lowered her eyes but not her head. "Are you mad, angry, pissed off?"

"If you mean, do I think 'Why me?' No, I've never thought those words, Ann. Not once. Rather, I say 'Why not me?' If this had to come into someone's life, why wouldn't it be mine? It sort of follows along with other things that have gone amiss, don't you think?"

I knew the other things she was referring to: a stillborn daughter and no other pregnancy, thereafter a husband who went off with another woman, and family gone. Parents whose death came so quickly in succession. An older sister who had died in childhood, another sister who lingered as an invalid for years after a debilitating stroke, and a brother, whom she loved dearly, died quickly of a heart attack not too many years ago. Sandy was the last of her siblings and her family now consisted of only two nieces and a nephew.

"God, it's got to be tough. It has to be hard to be without close family at this time." I said softly, able only to imagine what a void this must be.

Sandy nodded and our teary eyes locked. "Yeah, I don't seem to draw the winning numbers from the lottery of life, do I, Ann? I had expected another ten years at least. Most of my ancestors and my immediate family lived into their early 80s, so I wasn't concerned about checking out so soon."

"Shitty circumstances, I must say. Well, dear friend, what can I do to help you emotionally in the months ahead?"

She wouldn't go there with me, rather mentioned a shopping list she had ready, "Want to be my personal shopper this week? If I talk about the other I will cry, so why not just rub my legs."

I put her right leg in my hands and she asked, "When can you make your next visit?"

I learned that while ALS destroys the nerves that allow the limbs to move, the muscles do not die; they cramp and ache from lack of movement. Her legs were dead weight but had feeling, and as I massaged and flexed each leg, I'd see her eyes soften with relief. Those hours with her legs in my hands gave us some of our best talk time.

I learned more about ALS when I accompanied her on the clinic visits, the first in May and the second three months later in August. I heard her tell the doctors that she wanted no efforts to prolong her life, she just wanted to be as comfortable as one could be. Her wishes were honored. Along with the fear of choking was a dread of being alone. She wanted her days socially active and friends responded; her calendar showed a schedule of visitors for each morning, afternoon, and evening. She needed to look at that calendar and see that the days had little time without people. She kept us from being maudlin, feeling sorry for her, or pretending things would be different. Those numerous social visits, along with anti-depressants, kept her hours cheerful and light, avoiding for a while the dark horizon. As the final weeks approached, nursing aides were with her round the clock to ensure she received the trained assistance needed. They said Sandy's first words upon awaking were

"Damn it." We presumed it depicted her disappointment that another day was to be endured.

With all her generous ways, Sandy could be opinionated and determined, mostly bordering on stubbornness. It was a trait, I believe, that assisted her in handling this final assault on her being. Sandy, the disciplinarian, had her affairs in order, her medical instructions clear, her memorial planned and a eulogy written with Stan, her long-time neighbor and one of her best friends. She leaned on her friends to fill her days, to massage her legs, to do her bidding, and to fulfill her wishes of living a social calendar, as much as possible, to the end. And, to everyone's credit, her final good-byes were silently gracious, thoughtful, and loving.

As we were saying good-bye the last morning of my visit in May, Sandy said: "If you write my story, Ann, title it *She Went Out with Dignity.*"

And I added: "How about courage, grit, bravery, and grace?" The tears flowed profusely as our eyes fastened on each other, and I walked backwards out of her room.

Sandy's comment about writing her story lingered and I inquired by letter the following month if I'd been given permission to author her story with ALS. Sandy's answer was affirmative, and during my August visit, we were able to cover the early order of events when she first learned of her diagnosis. Knowing time was on the short end of the spectrum, we were restricted from the many sessions I would like to have had with her to tell her story verbatim. So may this story, crafted from a medley of her events, her friends, her faith, and her courage to face dying in character dignify her life and final days.

Chocolate Kisses

Sandy

I speak first with the woman at the front desk in my doctor's office. "Hello, this is Sandy Weisenburger and I was wondering what my test results were from the neurologist. It's been several weeks now and he said he'd be sending them to my primary doctor. I guess I expected a call."

While I took no call to be good news, my concern elevated yesterday when the home-care people informed me in an apologetic manner that they had to discontinue their services. The words "had to" indicated something had changed, although, it didn't make sense, since my strength had not returned from the back surgery of last spring.

"Mrs. Weisenburger, your doctor is still out for two more weeks on her extended vacation. I thought we had notified you that she would not be back until the end of the month."

"Yes, I knew she's been gone longer than usual, but I was hoping she'd be back by now or that I'd hear from someone."

"There is another doctor filling in for her . . . I can ask him to take your call."

After a short wait, a male voice without a name asks, "Can I help you?"

"Yes, I was wondering what the neurologist test indicated. I'm Sandy Weisenburger."

"Oh yes, I have that file here—the ALS diagnosis."

A black curtain dropped. My voice went silent. My mind dulled. I was numb with shock. It was the first time I'd heard anyone say ALS. Those letters were like a dagger to my mid-section. The pain welled up. I was stunned. I let the phone drop into its cradle. I was nauseated.

I felt lifeless, so futile; he hadn't even said my name or even his name. I was cold, so stricken; he hadn't even softened the sentence. I clutched the bars of the walker and dragged my useless foot into the bathroom. I leaned over the sink, tears sliding down my face, my throat gagging from bile. How could he have sentenced me so coldly, so carelessly, so impersonally, so finally?

Wipe the eyes, blow the nose, heave. I sobbed until I seemed empty of fluid. I stood up to face me in the mirror. A-L-S! So final. My insides felt as if I had a jungle of emotions gripped in an ugly vine of fear. I wanted liberation from the feelings of panic.

There is no recourse; there is no going back. I'm going to have to get on with it. I've lost the use of legs and there's more to go. Death is right here in front of me; the only thing on the agenda, and the way out looks pretty ugly. Where is my Dr. Kevorkian? I don't want life past this moment. Could I do suicide without assistance? I don't know.

Wipe the eyes, blow the nose, call Stan.

Stan

Sandy and I had been neighbors for over twenty-five years, the patio doors of our townhouses facing each other across a courtyard lawn. A path between our houses is well defined, one can see that the grass is as stubborn as the two of us—it keeps growing even though flattened by thousands of our footsteps. We've been there for each other through family celebrations and tragedies; a cat in one house was a pet in the other's; caretakers during vacations; chauffeurs when needed; our homes as bed and breakfast for each other's house guests; emotional support when times got tense; and now I was going to have to help her through her last and final crisis.

"Sandy, tell me what the doctor said."

"He just said ALS with no introduction, no compassion . . . just cold, hard words. How could a doctor be so cruel?" Sandy sobbed.

"What did you ask him?" I waited. "Did he want to see you?"

"I just hung up on him."

"That doesn't help much. You are going to have to talk with someone about it." I sat down on the couch across from her, "Sandy, for once I am at a loss as to what to say or do." I shook my head and looked away. I'm usually the calm one in an emergency, but this time my emotions were running amok. "I had a premonition that you were afflicted with more than a bad back but this is beyond anything I imagined. I never thought it would be anything that couldn't be corrected given time."

"Stan, I don't know what to do. I feel like a boxer who has just been knocked out of the ring. Do you suppose I could do suicide?"

"Sandy!" I jumped up moving away from the absurd idea. I turned to face her, "I won't go there with you. That's never an option in my mind nor my religion."

She put her head down and her body jerked with silent

sobbing. I went to my knees in front of her and put my hand over hers.

"I'm scared, Stan. I'm scared, so scared." Her voice trailed off into a whimpering wail.

"Sssh, sssh."

"I can't do this."

"Come on, let's just handle this evening for now, okay? I could call some friends in . . . would you like that?"

"Not yet. Would you make me a Manhattan?"

"Mid-afternoon?" I questioned. "I've never known you to drink mid-day, unless it was a very special occasion."

"Don't you think this is one hell of a special occasion? Far from a celebration but it sure is a whopper," she said through her sniffles. "Make it stiff, maybe I could get drunk so I can forget the whole day."

Her eyes held mine as she added, "Could you stay with me until tomorrow? I don't want to be alone."

"Yeah, I guess I could do the couch. What about tomorrow?"

"Maybe Mary Ann or Ruth. Would you call them?"

"Of course, but can Mary Ann leave her classroom of kids?"

"Probably not. If Ruth can't, maybe Patty. But, I'm not ready to tell her yet. I'll have to think of how and when. This will be an added burden with all the sickness she is facing in her family and with herself." Sandy sniffled. "Oh, Stan how can I tell anyone?"

"We don't have to decide that right now. Do you want anyone to come now?"

"I don't know. What do you think?"

"We could order in dinner, and I have a lovely bottle of Fume Blanc at the house, nice and delicate."

"I don't think I can eat and keep it down. And we can

forget the Manhattan. You're right, I don't drink my troubles away."

Wow, I didn't see this coming. I don't think I can talk about it right now either. First, we'll need a thorough understanding of the medical complications and prognosis. Sandy won't be looking for miracles. I think she doubts their existence—except those belonging to Jesus.

Marilyn

"Yoo-hoo, here's your favorite ditzy blonde." I called out as I walked into the house to find Sandy flushed with swollen red eyes, and Stan sitting silently across from her holding a box of Kleenex.

"What's happened?" I asked

"He says I have ALS—Lou Gehrig's disease."

"Who, Stan?"

"No," replied Stan. "She just heard the results from the neurology tests in a very blunt, insensitive manner."

"What? Who told you? How can we be so sure that's what you have? Let's go to Mayo," was my quick answer.

"Right now, let's get through this day," suggested Stan.

I went to put my arms around Sandy. "God, I can't believe this. I was hoping for something kinder."

Sandy grabbed Marilyn's hands, "Can you stay for the evening?"

"Of course. I wouldn't feel comfortable leaving."

"How about all night? I don't want to be alone." Her face was raw emotion.

I took her in my arms and held her as she sobbed. Stan put his head down into his hands and broke down.

I knew it. Something was not right. I'd known Sandy for twenty years, from our early days at General Mills, and could read her moods. She wasn't one to share her worries, but I'd felt for some time there was not good news behind the drop foot. I suspected it was serious and suspected it might be a neurological disease. I'd seen my mother have similar symptoms with Parkinson's.

I'd been Sandy's chauffeur for physical therapy sessions these last several months and noticed she was taking longer in raising her left leg high enough so the foot wouldn't drag. It seemed she had to make a conscious decision for each step, and it was an effort for her to get up and down the two front steps and in and out of the car. A few weeks ago, as we stood at the steps, Sandy said, "Marilyn, could you lift my right leg?"

"Sandy, that's your good leg, isn't it?"

"I know, but I need you to lift it. I can't."

"Does your doctor know about this?"

"No."

I knew Sandy had been calling the surgeon looking for answers as to why she was not getting better, but she'd been unable to get him on the phone. He seemed to be avoiding her. He did leave a message through the nurse that she should think about having another MRI. The nurse said Sandy would have to pick up some paper work at their office. I offered to do so, for I had another plan in mind.

"I'm not leaving this office until I speak with the doctor." I said as the receptionist handed me the papers.

"You don't have an appointment, do you?" she asked.

"No, but I am not leaving until I speak with him."

"Have a seat and I'll speak with the nurse."

"No, I'm standing right here until the doctor comes out."

She must have sensed my determination and urgency,

for the doctor flew out of the inner door shortly and took me to seats in the corner of the room. I gave him a direct message: "Doctor, you've got to talk with Sandy. She is not doing well and her leg strength is weakening. She's scared and she needs answers."

I never told Sandy what I did but she got a call, scheduled the MRI and the surgeon saw her immediately thereafter, proclaiming the surgery was successful.

Sandy

When had this affliction started? Was the first hint last year in London when my legs gave away and I fell from the steps of the tour bus?

No, the first indication was probably the drop foot condition that started early last year. My left foot wouldn't bend; it drooped and dragged as I walked, causing me to stumble and later to fall. I ignored the condition, my usual avoidance to possible bad news. Also, I wanted no hindrance to the upcoming trips; first the Celtic trip to England with Mary Ann and Carol and next to Peru with Mary. I wanted to achieve my life-long dream of climbing the ancient ruins. So, I made light of the fall in London and blamed the altitude of Machu Picchu for the intense fatigue and loss of limb strength I experienced. Apprehension escalated when I fell two months later in the cafeteria at the Chicago Art Institute, nearly banging my head on the table. My body ached so badly after that fall, and my friends who were with me strongly urged me to seek medical advice. But, still I put aside a doctor's visit. How determined I can be not to face what I don't want to know about.

And was this disease the underlying cause for the unbearable back pain that led me to have surgery this past March? Yet, the surgeon declared the operation a success and promised I'd get my strength back with therapy and walking. I was diligent with the therapy throughout the summer. It wasn't easy to get myself there twice a week on top of the four days I worked at the volunteer office at General Mills. I was dependent upon that awkward walker for moving about, but I was determined to be self-reliant. What a chore to get from my front door to the garage across the driveway, clopping along with the walker. I'd fold and stash it in the back seat while I hung on to the roof of the car for balance. The last gyration was to swing my butt around into the front seat, drag my left leg in, rest to catch my breath and then start the car.

Despite all the weeks of therapy, my strength did not improve. Friends thought I wasn't walking enough and angrily scolded me for not doing the prescribed exercises, even though I was. Stan threatened to remove all the furniture from the living room, making it into a walking gym. Marilyn seemed to be the only one on my side and would push back on those who chided me. I felt embarrassed when I went for my six-month check-up with the surgeon in September. The gist of our conversation can be summed up in a few words.

"I haven't experienced any improvement. Why am I not getting stronger? You can see by the therapist's report that I have not neglected my work-outs."

"Well, as I compare the MRI's, pre-surgery and post-surgery, everything is fine. You shouldn't need or be using the walker by now."

"Well, doctor, I am and I'd like to keep working with the therapist. Would you write an order for continuing my therapy three times a week?"

Soon after I fell over backwards as I was getting out of the car in the General Mills parking lot. Thankfully, someone saw what happened and came to set the walker upright and assist me to my feet. Then came the devastating day I returned home and couldn't get out of the car. An unwelcome inner signal sent a feeling of doom. I had arm strength to pull myself up, but my legs would not hold me; they were like dish rags. I fell back into the seat, crying and calling Stan on my cell phone to come help.

From then on, the best I could do was move the walker and drag the left leg. I was disgusted with myself, frustrated with the downhill trend, and blaming myself for no improvement, particularly since the surgeon had decreed, "you shouldn't need the walker anymore."

Stan

I'd seen a growing struggle play out within Sandy in this past year. There were so many periods of aloof silence, quiet times when Sandy kept to herself, the house darkened without a visible welcome sign, and her reply to any probing questions was "nothing." She disappeared emotionally, and in hindsight, I suspect she suspected something was seriously wrong. Others hinted of the falls that were happening but Sandy never spoke of them—not her style. If I pushed too hard, she'd give me her famous scowl or a deadly zinger meaning 'shut up.' We went to movies more often, her practice when a subject was to be avoided. To sit in a dark movie house and let a large screen override what she wished to avoid was typical Sandy. She wanted company, but watching a movie in a dark theater kept questions at bay and allowed her time to soft-pedal the issue. Undesirable events equaled bad news equaled calamity—all to be shunned for as long as possible.

She was so determined to make it to Peru. Nothing would stop her, although her health was unstable—high blood pressure, overweight, and the drop foot. What a big brave front she put up, attempting to fool others and herself. When I eventually heard from her friends that the fall in Chicago was serious, I saw her resolve for pretense give way. The back pain from the fall finally drove her to seek two opinions, and she gravitated to the doctor who held out the most promise, even though it was barely a 40/60 chance for success. I believe she laid a heap of hope on the surgery.

Marilyn

Sandy's last trip in 2002 and her last official convention took place in early summer, during the time she was still recuperating from back surgery. It was appropriate that Sandy be in attendance as it was an annual gathering for volunteers, and it was hinted that Sandy was to receive special recognition. I knew her friends from General Mills wanted her to be there, and I was more than willing to make that happen. After all, Sandy had long been unheralded as queen of volunteerism and now she was to be honored for her many years of leadership.

Stan helped me load the car with all of Sandy's special needs equipment and we headed for Duluth. I promised to be ever present by her side to attend to all requests, assist with walking and the walker and, if necessary, to do the walking when she couldn't. I did not want her to suffer the embarrassment of a fall. Sandy would have none of it. I was allowed to drive her to the convention hall and pick her up. She refused to take the walker with her, just the cane—a typical Sandy desire to keep things in her control, to herself, and to downplay any disability when it came to public appearance.

Since I didn't have a gate pass, I heard the convention news from the General Mills group of volunteers. Sandy was the star of the moment in honor of a lifetime of giving. Attention she had created for many others, but never sought for herself, was now focused on her. I could tell from the smile, the glow in her eyes, and occasional tear that she was touched deeper than she'd ever say. And, of course, I heard her usual, "I was only doing what needed to be done." She gave praise to all volunteers and especially to those who had worked so long and diligently with her. "I couldn't have done it without them." She never revealed to me the accolades she must have received. Our Sandy, never self-serving.

Stan

The days of summer moved into fall and I received more S.O.S. calls. Sandy would fall and have to crawl to the telephone. On one occasion, people who took her to therapy couldn't get her up the two steps into the house, and I found them on the outside sidewalk, holding her and crying. The drop foot got worse, and I began going over every night to help her up to her bedroom, her foot dragging, toe down, up each step. Sometimes I was by her side, other times I was holding her stable from behind. It's a wonder that we didn't both fall down the staircase. Finally, she agreed to setting up her bedroom downstairs with her usual hand off, "if you say so."

Her confidence was dented and reality was portraying a situation too awful to acknowledge. Simple movement was taking more effort; she sat for longer periods of time and neglected exercise. I turned to scolding and accused her of being lazy. She'd give me a look of a hurt kitten and say, "Do I really have to?" Neither one of us wanted to admit that her condition was worsening and that we were scared.

Sandy

By September 2002, seven months after surgery, I was totally dependent on my friends for transportation to therapy, household chores, and meals. I got up and down stairs to my bedroom on my butt or with Stan's help, but that was not to last much longer. I finally faced the question head on with my therapist.

"Why am I not getting any better?" I asked. "There's got to be a reason why there is no improvement."

The therapist gave a grave response. "With all the therapy and your persistent efforts, strangely, your muscles are getting weaker rather than stronger."

"How can that be? What else can I do? Where do I go from here?"

"I can't answer those questions. I'd like to call your surgeon and suggest more testing. Would that be okay with you?"

"Yes, whatever you can do to help me."

The surgeon sent me to a neurologist, who badly needed training in cordiality. He did an examination, asked questions and gave diagnosis with an indifferent, detached, aloof manner.

He was direct when he asked, "Do you know what spinal stenosis is?

"No, I don't."

"I believe that is what you have. Spinal stenosis is the narrowing of the spaces in the spine, resulting in pressure on the spinal cord and nerve roots. It is an aging process and does not reverse itself. Correction involves a lot of delicate surgery and doesn't always hold full promise of success."

"That's not very encouraging."

He sent his diagnosis to the surgeon, who responded

with "Can't be" and ordered another MRI. This would be the third one, and this time, the procedure could not be completed. I was unable to lie still for the one hour that was needed. Painful muscle spasms involuntarily moved and twitched my legs.

The technician told me, "You have to hold still."

"I can't hold still, the spasms come on their own. They don't stop."

"The MRI can't be done if you move. We'd have to start over each time."

"So be it. I can't stop the spasms."

God, what is happening? Where is this leading? I'm scared. Nothing seems to be going well. I'm confused; the doctors are not giving good answers nor comforting words. How bad is this going to be? Something is terribly wrong. I'm not feeling that luck is on my side.

Back to the surgeon who ordered a different test to be done by a neurologist. I told him I would never go back to the rude-mannered doctor. Insensitive men! How I wished I could talk with the female doctor who'd I'd been with for years, but she was on her month-long vacation. What a bummer; everything just seemed to get worse.

Along with another examination with yet another doctor was an electromyogram (EMG) to determine the health of my body's nerves and muscles. This test involved inserting electrodes into muscles and measuring the electrical signals. My words to the neurologist were, "Ugh, I detest needles. I can't watch. I'm going to keep my eyes closed." Needles went into my arms, legs, and spine. I clenched my mouth, held my breath making my cheeks puff with air, expelling each time the needle was withdrawn. *I pray the results from this test determine what's wrong; I surely don't want to go through this again.*

When they'd finished with my body, the doctor said, "You can open your eyes." I let out a sigh of relief thinking the testing was finished. But instead, the doctor stood in front of me holding a long ugly needle, ready to do the last insertion, giving me firm instructions to hold still. The needle entered under my chin into the tongue from the underside. I was tense and unable to hold back tears. He patted my shoulder. No diagnosis was offered that day. I was to hear the dreadful words ALS from Dr. No-Name who bluntly gave me the test results several weeks later.

Stan

Deb and I brought Sandy home that afternoon. The testing had exhausted the three of us. Sandy's strength was simply used up, gone, kaput. She was unable to go up the two steps into her house and crumbled in a heap on the sidewalk. I held her upright as best I could as Deb went to find assistance from a neighbor. We managed to get Sandy through the door but not without a struggle. I realized for the first time my limitations in helping her.

This appointment with needles noticeably changed Sandy. I marked that afternoon as a turning point. Sandy's spunk was forever altered; her fighting spirit seemed to have died on the entrance to her home. Little did I comprehend how different life would become in the months ahead.

Sandy

Now I had the verdict, but what did the sentence entail. A process had begun in my body over which I would never have any control. How long? What conditions? Where do

I go? Who oversees my physical health? How much pain? What can I expect? What would the final days be like? I opened these questions with my closest friends, none of whom were familiar with ALS.

One option seriously considered was to get a second opinion from Mayo Clinic. My friend, Barb, working through her medical network got an appointment in Rochester, and we understood that I would be subject to examinations again and re-testing to confirm the diagnosis. Another friend, Peggy, offered the name of a doctor for whom her husband, also a neurologist, had a high degree of trust and confidence. And, all the time, I wanted the familiar presence of my own doctor but that didn't overshadow my insistent need to know the full implications *now.* So I opted to see Peggy's doctor first, holding a visit to Mayo as an alternative.

He proved to be Dr. Wonderful! First, he gave up his lunch hour to meet with me immediately. "While I ordinarily rely on and prefer my own tests, I trust the results I have in hand. They are thorough and obviously conclusive," he told us.

Secondly, the story he had to tell was done with compassion, kindness, and dignity, a rarity I seldom saw in men. He was a doctor of warm nature telling a cheerless and dismal story. At the end of an hour, he stood up, put his hand on my shoulder and gave apologies, "I am sorry that I had to give you such hopeless and hard news. It's a tough road ahead of you." His gesture was the most compassionate touch I'd had from the medical profession.

"Don't be nice to me, or I'll breakdown and start sobbing."

"Guess I'd better get a tissue then."

As I wiped my eyes, I told him, "Thank you for your

kindness in giving up your lunch hour for me. You've helped me understand what's happening to me and the decisions I face."

My friends, Barb and Deb, had gone with me—a good idea, so that all the specifics would be captured. We left quietly and in a state of disbelief. Our conversation was stilted, and we parted to our separate homes. There seemed to be nothing to say. The sentence had a finality that could not be dismissed.

I sat alone at home contemplating what I'd heard. The doctor had been specific and the disease defined.

"We do not know why a person gets ALS but we do know the process. Over time, both the upper and lower motor neurons degenerate or die, ceasing to send messages from the brain. As the damaged neurons shrivel, they pull away from the muscles. Unable to function, your muscles gradually weaken, waste away, and twitch. Eventually the ability of the brain to start and control voluntary movement is lost."

"I'll become a prisoner in my body. Is that what it's like?"

"That's a close enough description."

"How long does this take?"

"Well, the rate of degeneration varies from patient to patient. The disease seems to have a distinct rate of progress in each person; if it starts fast, it typically continues a rapid downtrend. If it starts slow, the progress is slow."

"I know what the end is, but how does my body get there?"

"When muscles in the diaphragm and chest wall fail, patients lose the ability to breathe. That's when you'll need ventilator support. Because ALS affects only motor neurons, the disease does not impair a person's mind, personality, intelligence, or memory. Nor does it affect a person's ability to see, smell, taste, or recognize touch. Body massage will feel good to you and therapeutic exercises will help to maintain mobility of your limbs."

"Now for the hard question, doctor." A pause. "How long?"

"I know that is a tough question, and it has a rough answer. Typically three to five years, although some patients survive for ten or more years."

"I don't want to linger that long without mobility. My greatest fear is of suffocation. I don't want to choke or fight for breath." I had to fight back tears and hold tight on my emotions.

"We don't let that happen. You'll have respiratory support, both equipment and medicine, when the time comes."

Dr. Wonderful helped us sort out our choice of Minneapolis or Mayo. He said it was important which clinic I choose because all future visits, check-ups, therapy prescriptions, equipment, hospital visits would have to be in the chosen city. He wanted me to consider the drive time and inconvenience of getting from Minneapolis to Rochester, particularly in the later months. He pointed out that one of the best men in the medical field for ALS was right here at Hennepin Clinic, and he reportedly had a very competent team working with him. My final decision was to stay with Hennepin Clinic, which proved to be a wise decision—their medical team was equally as good as my experience with Dr. Wonderful.

Patty

"Patty, can you come over?" I heard Sandy breathe in a child-like tone.

"What's up? Are you back from the doctor?" I inquired.

"Yes, and the verdict is awful. Can you come over? I need a friend with me."

"I bet I don't want to hear the verdict. How bad is it?"

"It's the worst. There's no reprieve. It's ALS."

Silence

"Are you there, Patty?"

"Yes."

"Please come stay with me. I can get some one to pick you up. I don't want you to drive."

"No, let me throw a few things together and I'll call a cab. Are you alone now?"

"Yes, Barb just left on an errand and will be back in a few minutes."

"I'm coming as soon as I can. I'm so sorry, dear friend. Hang on, I'll be there."

The shock sent me reeling. In a daze, I called for a cab and quickly slung some clothes and items into an overnight bag, for I knew Sandy would not want me to leave. Thank God, Stan lives across the court. He will help in sorting this out and determine what to do. This is a terrible blow on top of my sister's recent illness. In forty-five minutes I was on my way.

I arrived just as Barb was getting ready to leave; her parents were waiting for her at their doctor's office. She'd helped Sandy to the bathroom and had wheeled her back into the living room near the bed. "Do you need help in getting Sandy on the bed?" she asked. We got Sandy to a sitting position on the edge of the bed as Barb blew a kiss and flew out the door. "I'll be in touch tomorrow. Glad you're here with her, Patty."

As I leaned over and lifted Sandy's legs onto the bed, we

were face-to-face, eyeball-to-eyeball. With her words, "Can you imagine what this will be like?" our tears could not be held back. We looked at each other and cried, Sandy holding on to me like a baby. I heard Sandy finally giggle.

"The tears are running into my ears and tickle as they go down the tube. Hand me a Q-tip," she said, wrinkling up her nose.

"Let's hope we won't have to do that again," were Sandy's final words about crying.

I remained with her for three days and nights, helping her contact people and arranging a new calendar of activities. Sandy and I had met at General Mills back in 1958 when we worked in the same office. She was a happy, cheerful person with a very positive outlook. It was great to work with her. She always did more than was called for and made it fun doing so. Nothing was ever half-ass with Sandy; if a thing was to be done, it was to be done superbly. She was married at the time, and I got to know her and her husband when we joined twenty other General Mills employees for a tour of Europe. Her outgoing personality added a lot of zest and energy to the group, and she instigated quite a few delightful side excursions during those three weeks. One night it was a naughty show with can-can dancers.

We became closer friends after her divorce, a bitter and painful experience for her, and one that altered her personality forever. The bitterness flowed over into a negative attitude and lowly perception of herself. I, along with other co-workers, urged her to seek professional counseling, and the sessions did help over time, although Sandy never returned to her earlier optimistic attitude. Those personal struggles left indelible low marks in her opinion of men and her fortunes in life. By nature, she was fiercely loyal, and it followed that she had expected the same from others. Her husband's infidelity was a grievous wound for Sandy.

I bet that she'll see this new and unwanted twist to her life as a bad roll of the dice—another piece of rotten luck. She so often expected the worst to come her way and I expect to hear her say, "See I told you so." But underneath, she is strong and resilient, and she'll step up to take control. She won't let this sink into a self-pity party. I trust my health holds strong for she'll want all of us with her. She's always been there for me, through my heart attacks and other hospitalizations. I won't let her down.

Sandy

Independence, valued so highly by me, is being relinquished bit by bit. Much to my liking, people come in and out of my house all day: home health care, breakfast with Stan, friends and church members doing the other daily meals, someone always remained for the evening. I can't get up the stairs to my bedroom anymore so a couple from church, Louiva and Jim, brought in a twin bed for downstairs. The living room has become my single living space. My daytime confined to a wheelchair and nighttime to the bed. With assistance, I can still take the few steps to get from one seat to another. Ruth, a retired nurse and friend, helps me with my shower and dressing each morning, and two young members of the church, Amy and Vicki, take turns sleeping here at night. When I awake and call out, I find them often asleep with a pillow on the floor by my bed or curled up in the loveseat across the room. God love 'em. They worry that they will not hear me from the upstairs bedroom.

I am embarrassed with this new role. I am an imposition on others. I don't want it. It is so hard to accept, but it's going to be down hill all the way. I will have to let go, damn it! I never imagined that the control of my body would not be in my command. What a shitty situation. And where would I be without all these wonderful people? I need to get a grip on a new perspective if I want to ease the burden, for them and for me. Time to pray, Sandy.

I'm standing at the edge of life, not wanting to fall into the darkness of despair. How do I want to live the rest of my days? I don't want to be moved into the past tense; I want to stay present tense. I want to live every moment to the most that each moment can be. I want to be in charge of my life as long as possible. I need my dignity, and I can maintain it by tending to my affairs.

There's lots to do: the move, choosing a nursing home, finding a Realtor, arranging for an estate sale, sorting through my household possessions, planning a memorial service, getting my affairs into final order. And, I have to count on my friends to share with me each day whatever joys of life might remain for me. *Have faith Sandy.*

Sandy

My brother, Lawrence, always liked to refer to me as a good North Dakota gal who expressed her love through food and hospitality. I found his description neither unbrotherly nor untrue, just not sure that the trait was exclusive to our home state.

Holidays were special occasions and were always full of preparation to make them a celebration. Thanksgiving Day honored a time-old tradition among my extended family of friends in Minneapolis. We typically gathered at my house each year, enjoying a good part of the day and evening with spirited conversation, wine, and turkey dinner. Stan and my nephew, Larry, prepared what was to be our last Thanksgiving celebration. Stan had found my prized Christmas dishes stored carefully on a closet shelf and had secretly taken them to his house. I loved those Mikasa dishes with the Christmas tree pattern. They were pricey and I wouldn't indulge in buying the full set at one time, rather place settings had come to me from friends, either as a birthday or Christmas gift.

"Gee, are you thinking that I won't be here at Christmas?" I sarcastically tossed at them when I saw the table set with the dishes.

"No, we thought they'd beautify our holiday table."

"Reminds me of a last supper."

"Cut the pessimism," came their reply.

Stan added, "I've decided that all your meals until your move should be served on these cherished dishes. Better than them being stacked in a box waiting to be sold."

"Besides, who better to enjoy them than us?" said Larry.

"Bon appetite," as everyone raised wine glasses.

Until my move in January those lovely holiday dishes graced the table every day. I must admit it did put a gourmet touch to the meals shared with so many friends during the last two months in my home.

Glyn

I came into Sandy's extended family for holiday celebrations about eight years ago and found out quickly that everyone had a task to do in preparation for holidays. My assignment was polishing the silver tea service. I'm not sure exactly how this chore fell upon me, but I've been doing it for the last six years. Polishing day became a social occasion by itself—I did the work, Sandy did the cooking, Stan did the monologue.

"Why do I do this? Why do I feel obligated to clean this silver set twice a year?" I put on a playful pout like a little kid.

"Maybe because it's an occasion for Manhattans and dinner," Sandy suggested.

"I could think of better reasons than that, as if we needed a reason for booze and food."

"I think it's a piece of Sandy's ritual to ensure that her male slaves remain obligated to her at least twice a year," teased Stan.

"You're not angling for an invite to a tea party, are you?" Sandy chimed in.

"Why not?" We always laughed and pestered Sandy every time the tea service was put back on display. "When do I get invited to a tea party?" I asked. "In fact, when do you ever have one?"

"Never you mind, it's women only."

"Sandy, we are going to crash one of your female parties one of these days."

"Better wear hats and gloves if you are coming to my tea party."

At our last Thanksgiving dinner, Sandy offered her prized tea service to any one of us. "I won't need it anymore." Words we would hear often over the next two months.

"Count me out," said Patty. "I dropped out of the tea party circuit years ago."

"Don't know who I'd be serving tea to," I said. "Think I can give up the polishing chore."

"I have my mother's tea set. I don't need two," added

Mary Ann. "However, the church women might be inclined to do tea parties."

"Yeah, why not give it to your church?" suggested Stan.

"I think not," snapped Sandy, as she turned to her nephew. "How about you, Larry? You can make the decision within the family."

"It's not a family heirloom. Maybe we'll sell it."

"Over my dead body." A quip said quickly in jest, but it dampened our conversation.

Amy and Vicki

We came late into Sandy's circle of friends. She was not a stranger to us, however. We'd watched her from a distance as members of the United Church of Christ and often remarked about Sandy's charismatic personality. She always seemed to be prominent in church functions. Along with the congregation, we knew that she was instrumental in organizing the fundraising projects, which were highly successful, for the church. She appeared to do it all so effortlessly, with a big smile and a happy disposition.

"Are you two friends up to doing a good deed?" asked Pastor Carol one Sunday morning after services.

"Well, depends on what the good deed is," we answered.

"It has to do with Sandy Weisenburger. You know her, don't you?"

"Not real well," replied Vicki. "I know she was here when I took on the position of custodian for the church. When was that? Two or three years ago? We dealt with each other when church events were in the works. She always knew what and how she wanted things."

"Golly, one would have to be blind not to notice that she is very active in the church," added Amy. "The last potluck dinner she organized was the best. What's up now? Does she have another project she needs help with?"

"Not exactly the type you're probably thinking. You've no doubt noticed that Sandy has been in a wheelchair lately?" asked Carol.

"Yes, and before that she was using a walker, wasn't she? I heard she was recuperating from back surgery."

"Well, her physical condition is far worse than that. She was recently diagnosed with ALS."

"No, how terrible! That's Lou Gehrig's disease."

"God, that's an awful disease."

"Yeah, not with good prospects and it's coming on fast. I've seen a big change in these last couple of months. She's still at home but in need of care, day and night. Her days seem filled with friends. One of them is a nurse who comes every morning to help her shower and dress, and others are fixing her meals. In fact, many of the cooks are from our church."

"That's what's so great about this church, the generosity of the congregation. Such a healthy attitude here," said Vicki.

"You must be proud to be pastor, Carol," added Amy.

Carol nodded, "I am. No one seems to hesitate to give a helping hand. I think that's a function of who they are rather than who their pastor is. Back to Sandy . . . I got to get goin', someone is waiting to talk with me. It's the night hours that she has no one, from maybe eight or nine until the nurse arrives in the morning. I'm thinking that you both have flexible work hours. I know you do here at church, Vicki. How about you Amy?"

"Working my own schedule as a therapist does give me some options. Think I could move night appointments to daytime. Do you know how long she'd need us, Carol?"

"I understand from Mary Ann, who saw Sandy yesterday, that maybe a little over two weeks, at least until the end of December."

"That could work. We're staying in town this holiday and decorating our own house," Vicki said. "We were planning a few parties, but we can hold 'em on the week-end days or push 'em into January."

"Well think it over. There'd be sleep interruptions, although, I don't know how often Sandy does wake up. But, at your young age, you probably still operate at high gear with little sleep," Carol said with a grin. "Here's the telephone number, and I suggest you visit her. I bet she'll know who you are."

We talked off and on for the rest of the day and finally decided we had no reason not to offer our help. We'd often mentioned how we'd liked to get to know Sandy better, and now here was the opportunity. Although, we were unaware of the sadness to be experienced.

We called Sandy and went to her house the next evening. We got to meet her nephew, Larry, a quiet guy who sat and listened to our conversation and thanked us when we left. It was evident that she was in need of assistance. We learned more of her diagnosis and her reluctance, which later we knew was fear, to be alone during the night. She needed help getting in and out of bed and the wheelchair, as her legs were lifeless. Sandy told us she was a night owl, her bedtime was around midnight, and that our sleep would be interrupted when she needed to turn her body or get to the bathroom. We assured her we were prone to late hours ourselves. I think she liked the fact we were young.

Our decision was instant and unanimous. Yes, we wanted to help her, not only for all she had done to build our church community but to get to know this neat lady.

She had a welcoming aura about her that was irresistible. Later, we saw how true this was; seldom was she without friends in her company. Their conversations were speckled with old-time stories full of fun and laughter. It sounded like she'd been the spark of life.

We began our nightly sleepover the week of Christmas when her niece Myra left for home in North Dakota. We alternated nights until her California friends arrived in January to help with the big move.

Larry

Aunt Sandy and I would not have our annual baking ritual this holiday, and I was glad that she didn't ask me to be the single baker for her Christmas rosettes. It wouldn't have been a happy occasion for either of us, although I know it was difficult for her to let her friends down. Her holiday goodie boxes were a source of pride.

Making dozens of the rosette cookies had been a ten-year tradition for us, typically a long day on a weekend close to Christmas. The dining room table, extended to full length, would be covered with rosettes, the round delicate flaky pastry in the shape of a rose. After the kitchen work came the careful wrapping of the rosettes into holiday boxes (usually a dozen per box) for hand delivery to Minneapolis friends.

She had another equally delightful Christmas ritual—making caramels, hand wrapping them, and mailing boxes to friends who lived out of town. Anyone not leaving the city over the holidays would be targeted as kitchen helpers for the caramel sessions. I usually was relieved of this.

Friends might receive rosettes or caramels before they even received her holiday cards; those got addressed on Christmas Eve. One would ask, "Why send a late

Christmas card?" Her response, with a twinkling eye, was that her holiday greetings would be remembered because hers came after all the rest. I suggested once, "Might it be a cop-out for procrastination, or is it vanity?" She shook her finger, "Don't be nasty now, or Santa will skip your house."

Mary

"Yes, Sandy, I can get away in January to help you move. What's the plan?"

"Bless Larry and Karen. They did the legwork of visiting assisted-living places, and have honed in on two options. I'm getting close to choosing one."

"So soon?"

"'Fraid so. I can't live between two floors anymore. My legs are weakening, and I don't have much mobility."

"Who's with you?"

"Well, Ruth is still helping me in the morning. And Deb and Marilyn during the day. Others, also. And, of course, Stan is always cross the way."

"Aren't the girls from church with you at night?"

"Yes, they are so sweet. I woke up the other night and found Amy sleeping on the floor by my bedside. They are so conscientious and worried they won't hear my call from the upstairs bedroom. I've asked them to continue on, but it's not going to work after the holidays."

"Do they have to sleep on the floor? Where are the couches?"

"They are over by the wall, but remember they are two-seaters."

"How about I fly in after New Year's. Think we could get the job done in seven days? How many of us are helping?"

"Oh, I was thinking you'd stay three weeks."

"Golly, Sandy, I can't be away from my clients for that long."

"I'll pay your salary."

"For Christ's sake—like I'd feel right doing that."

"Three weeks isn't very long. You can do it. Just this one last time."

"Sandy, Sandy. Don't push me so." I said with a heavy sigh. "I was with you two weeks helping you after your back surgery, and I'll want to have some time available to return to Minneapolis later on."

"Really, why can't I hire you for longer?"

"No, Sandy, you are not hiring me," I said emphatically. "I've got a travel business that's pretty demanding. You know that. I'll try to work out two weeks. Okay?"

"Okay, but I really would like you to stay longer."

"What's new, you always do."

It was 1963 and I was in a hospital bed when I received the call from Sandy that launched our friendship.

"Hello, Mary, this is Sandy Weisenburger. I wanted to call and say how sorry I am to hear of your loss."

The name didn't register with me, but her next words answered my question.

"You might remember me. It was last spring at the ESA meeting of our two chapters. Remember, we were together on two committees, the By-laws and Nominations. We butted heads on a couple of things."

"Yeah, it was the By-laws, wasn't it? Due structure, I think."

"Whatever. I was with your Chapter President yesterday, and she told me that you were in the hospital."

"Yes, and she must have told you why."

"Guess that's why I felt the urge to call. I too had a stillbirth, and I remember how painful the loss was. I needed to reach out to you. Can I come visit?"

Wow, I was touched. I wanted to get to know this stranger who was so thoughtful to make such a call. Our friendship was immediate and was pretty solid by the time I moved to New York in 1970. Sandy and I shared more than the loss of our only pregnancies; we were support to each other as our marriages fell apart, mine while I was still in Minneapolis and hers after I left for New York. She was there when my parents died a month apart and I when her parents died a few years later, only eight weeks apart. It seemed we were in lockstep with our life experiences.

I moved to Chicago in 1976, giving a shorter travel distance between us until my move to California in the mid-80s. Both of us had our eyes on exotic places we wanted to see in our lifetime, and our bags were ready for travel, always. Our first trip began when Sandy called me in New York and said, "Want to go to Greece?"

A lot of convenience and opportunities opened for us after I became a travel agent in 1987. From then on, we did one or two trips a year. Our birthday presents to each other were secretly purchased during a trip. The opal pendant she bought for me in Australia is one of my favorites and brings compliments from women and men alike.

God, I'm going to miss her. How can we ever say good-bye? I'm not going to handle all this very well and not sure that she can do much better. She'll not want to talk about the bad stuff. Neither will I. Knowing Sandy, a lot will remain unsaid. I can only presume what she is going through. Damn it, I'd better go for the three weeks; she's pushing too hard not to have it matter. And, it isn't like another time is coming around. What's a client compared to Sandy?

Christmas Greetings from Sandy

I need to let you know this is the last Christmas greeting you will receive from this address. I have been diagnosed as having ALS (amyotrophic lateral sclerosis) or Lou Gehrig's disease.

It seems to be progressing very swiftly, so I need to move to a facility where I can have assistance 24/7. I have no idea where that might be. Have checked a couple of places but no luck so far. I am receiving help with every meal and other chores from scores of friends and family.

At this time only my legs and feet are affected, so I have no clue how long I will be able to write and otherwise communicate. This could be the last time you hear from me—but please know you will be in my thoughts often.

The first date I can see the ALS specialist is January 2nd. I hope to know more after that three-hour appointment. Although they say each case progresses differently, so maybe they won't tell me much.

I'm so glad I took two nice trips last year. Spent a few weeks in the British Isles in the summer, and then fulfilled a long-time dream by seeing Machu Picchu in the fall. Even went white-water rafting in Peru—which is quite a stretch for me. But it was certainly an experience to remember.

Mary, my long-time friend and travel companion, is coming to Minneapolis for three weeks in January to help me clean out thirty years' worth of accumulation in my townhouse. How do we get so much "stuff?" And what are we to do with it? Guess I'll find out.

My wish for each of you is good health in the years ahead, for if we have our health, we have everything.

Blessings on you all in this special season!

Patty

We were sitting at the dining room table, sorting through holiday wrapping paper and ribbons. While our conversation usually avoided anything about ALS, I had found an interesting item worth mention.

I began with, "Newsweek had an article about a medical clinic in Mexico that caught my attention."

"Yeah, in what way?"

"It tells about what seems to be miracle cures with different non-medicinal treatment."

"Like voodoo?"

"No, silly, herbal wraps, injections, tonics . . ."

She cut me off. "Patty, what validity does that have?"

"Well, surprisingly, a lot of clients are claiming cures, some with validation by their state-side doctors."

"Gotta be mostly cancer, right?"

"No, surprisingly again, they cite improvements with a number of neurological diseases."

"Do they specifically mention ALS?"

"One patient is there now, and they claim he can stand again by himself."

"So, what's the point? Are you suggesting I should traipse off to some quack in Mexico?"

"They say they have legit doctor titles. One has to wonder, what's to lose?"

"Maybe a lot of friends."

"But what if you'd keep your mobility longer?"

"Yeah, 'what if's' are just that . . . 'what if's' . . . Tell me, would you go down with me?"

"No, you know I can't travel anymore."

"Just think, we could take the cure together," she said with a hint of sarcasm.

"We'd witness two miracles, then," I laughed.

"Only a Catholic would count on miracles."

"Look, I didn't bring the topic up to start an argument. Just an interesting option worth discussing."

"Well, think I'll stay with American medicine."

"Suppose this does sound pretty off the wall to you and pretty risky."

"Let's be realistic, Patty. I think it's best to stay with the hand I've been dealt. Don't think I'm going to draw any wild card that's goin' to change my condition."

"Wish we could." We shrugged our shoulders and reached for a box to wrap.

Stan

Our little group gathered for our last Christmas dinner, which was served on the cherished holiday dishes. My father was over from Dakota and had always been a welcome guest in our family of friends. He and Sandy had been together many times over the years, and they enjoyed talking politics and the old days of North Dakota. Sandy always reminded Dad that North Dakota had a twenty-year-long streak of voting Republican in the presidential races from 1948 to 1988. And Dad would retort, "Yes, except for 1964 when Johnson took the vote." Dad was one of few Democrats Sandy treated as if Republican. Patty and I were the other two that I know of.

Sandy put her best efforts into making this last holiday special for all of us: Christmas carols playing, her collection of crystal trees on display, and gifts out of her home for everyone. Patty had helped her box and wrap the presents and claimed that the bin of paper and ribbons was empty. Our presents contained pieces of crystal glass from Europe, silver platters from England, stained glass cocktail picks from Italy, a cloisonné bar set from China, sea shell jewelry from Florida, treasures from her travels thoughtfully chosen for her holiday family. It was poignant and sentimental.

Amy

I arrived on Christmas night around eight-thirty to find a house full of people just finishing their Christmas party. Walking into a full house was not different than any other night. Sandy had friends with her at all hours. Old co-workers from General Mills were there most evenings, making coffee—the pot was in use constantly. I could see why Sandy was a night owl; she was never caffeine free. Friends didn't come empty handed, and their food offerings on the kitchen counter and in the refrigerator provided sumptuous evening snacks.

"Get a plate of food and a drink and let me introduce you to this motley crew," Sandy suggested.

It was easy to join in with their social hour, which typically went past ten o'clock. When the final goodnights were said, Sandy and I watched the evening news or a video, our entertainment as I massaged her legs and feet.

Our final conversations, after turning out the lights, were the best times. She'd ask about my work and career, and I'd ask her about her travels. She'd let me choose the country. Afterwards, Vicki and I regretted that we hadn't taped those travelogues.

Ann Wade

Glyn

It was New Year's Eve, an hour before the stroke of midnight and 2003 when Stan and I returned to his house after a black tie and tux benefit. In the dark we looked across the patio to see a full celebration in process: every light on, music playing, women moving about. This was the night we crashed one of Sandy's parties. With paper hats strapped on under our chins, red ribbon tied around our torsos in a bow, ornaments hanging from our wrists, a wine bottle and glass in hand we tramped across the snowy path blowing noise makers. They didn't hear us and only saw us when we had our noses pressed to the sliding door.

Sandy made us wait outside in the cold as she asked for a show of hands for inviting us in. We won thumbs up. The rest of the night was full of songs, laughter, eating, drinking, but I noticed no one ever said, "Happy New Year" or make a resolution.

Sandy

My nephew Larry and niece Karen scouted for accommodations I needed now and later. They finally had two homes for me to visit, narrowed down from an original list of ten locations. We visited both facilities. The first was so large—over five hundred beds—and not appealing to me. When I toured the second, Jones-Harrison, I knew I'd found the place I'd like. It was a solid, old, intimate establishment with attractive decor, amenities, and reputation. It was located on Cedar Avenue in a quiet, low-traffic residential area and a convenient central location for my visitors to find me. Jones-Harrison had one bedroom apartments with on-call nursing, and a wing with full nursing care which I would need in due time. And, the clincher was the denomination for Sunday services held on premises. I still would be attending a United Church of Christ conducted by a woman who was well known by Carol, the pastor of our church in Robbinsdale.

"We have a long waiting list for the nursing-care wing. I can't say how long it would be for a room to come available," said Margaret, the staff person who met with us.

"I would be willing to pay a move-in fee," I replied. Margaret gave me a dubious look.

"Or could I pay to get on a preferred list?"

Margaret chuckled, "It's never been our practice to allow a client to buy their way in."

"I guess I am glad to hear that, just thought I'd ask. Seriously, what can be done, as I am sold on Jones-Harrison?"

"Well, this might work. There is a one-bedroom apartment available and then, as a resident, moving to the nursing-care unit on the third floor would be just a matter of the next opening," said Margaret.

"Could we see the apartment?" asked Karen.

As we went down the hallway, the thought of having an apartment was attractive, for it would allow me to retain some semblance of independent living. I still had Ruth, a friend and retired nurse, who I'd hired several months ago for personal assistance. She had been coming to the house each day to help me bathe, shampoo, and dress in the morning and then returned to ready me for bed in the evening. There was no reason why she wouldn't continue do so.

"In the apartment unit," said Margaret, "we have staff for medical care as needed but not much personal assistance. I presume that you can care for yourself and get to the dining room for meals."

"Yes." I replied quickly. Larry and Karen both turned my way and I gave them a slight shake of my head.

We left Jones-Harrison with a done deal and plans to move in before February first.

"Sandy, I think I heard a little white lie." Karen said once we were in the car.

"Like what?"

"Who's going to help you in the bathroom during the day?"

"Ruth is."

"She doesn't stay all day," Larry challenged.

"Well, maybe I'll hire her for more hours. And friends will be with me."

"What about night hours? Vicki and Amy won't be with you."

"I'll cut my liquids."

"You'll be mad as hell when you pee the bed," Karen scolded.

"Come on, kids, let me try it, will you."

"Well, at least you'll be teed up for a room on the nursing floor," were Larry's last words.

Vicki

In very quick order Amy and I could see that Sandy had been a consummate hostess, and she continued that role even though her physical condition kept her off her feet. She usually offered a choice for evening entertainment—video movies, cribbage, jigsaw puzzles, or what became our favorite, her albums of travel photos. We had shied from traveling abroad, mostly due to cold feet of the unfamiliar rather then the lack of interest in other cultures.

Sandy became our travel guide as she took us through her pictures of Turkey, Russia, Greece, Egypt, South America, Australia, China, and England—her favorites of world trips. She gave us so many tips to allay our fear about overseas travel. If she could have planned another trip, we both knew she would have included us.

Amy and I were both there the night Sandy recounted her trip to Peru, the last one with her friend Mary. As she tucked the photos back into an envelope, Sandy said, "Well that's the end of my travels. Put these in the box, Vicki, and throw them away."

"You mean trash all of these?" I asked incredulously.

"Yes, it's ended. It's over. There'll be no more." She sat still, as if caught in memories.

Amy looked at me, raised her eyebrows and hinted, "But maybe someone else would like these pictures—your traveling companions."

"No, what's over is over. I don't want to see them again."

"We can't throw away your memories," I replied.

"They're of no importance now." Sandy began to cry.

Amy went to her side immediately, "It's okay, Sandy. This is hard."

She knelt and held her hands.

It was an emotional evening, probably not good for Sandy's health but I think it might have been a catharsis. There are times when the tension has to be released. Sandy could cry in front of us, maybe because we were the new set of friends with no history and no façade she had to maintain.

"Please don't stop coming to see me," Sandy pleaded. "Do you know how to find Jones-Harrison?"

"We do and you couldn't keep us away."

"Good. You are my angels, and angels are always there, aren't they?"

"You grant us too much, Sandy. These hours have been our privilege." I said.

"Wonder why we didn't get closer before now, after all you are the custodian of the church, Vicki. It can't be because you and Amy are many years younger than me, I've always gravitated towards younger people."

"I might have held back," I offered. "You are pretty awesome in the things you get accomplished. Quite a few of the congregation spoke so highly of your talents. Maybe we were shy and admired you from a distance rather than stepping into your circle."

"Well, shame on the three of us, right?" replied Sandy.

"Think I've learned a lesson," Amy said. "Vicki, we should join more church projects. Wonder what other friendships we may be missing."

"Amy, with your background, you'd be a great addition to the BeFrienders group," suggested Sandy.

"That seemed so much like the therapy work I do every day."

"Not always so. Sometimes people just need a companion for a bit. Maybe to do fun things, or a chore or two, or have a meal together."

"We could organize the next potluck," Vicki proposed.

"There you go. Do it."

"Okay, Miss Inspiration." I gave her a salute.

"Glad you both came tonight. Amy, in the top drawer of the credenza you'll find a long box. I want to give you something of mine."

Sandy opened a velvet-lined box containing beautiful pieces of jewelry with carved faces. She told us how she had become fascinated with cameos when she was a little girl. Two of them were her grandmother's, handed down to her mother and then to Sandy. She laid those aside and told us, "These belong in the family, but please select one of the others that you'd like."

"Sandy, you've been kind enough already with the check you gave us," Amy said. "It was our intention to do a good deed, not be for hire and gifts."

"Girls, girls, you earned those few dollars. I know I forced you to take it but as I said 'give me leeway,' I still have the errors of pride and vanity."

"Jeez, these are beautiful and some look antique. Do they have a story?" I asked.

"Except for these two family cameos, the rest I bought through the years at antique stores or estate sales."

Sandy watched Amy pick up a blue locket. "That's an unusual cameo. It's appealing, isn't it?"

"Yes. I like the shape of it and the blue background is gorgeous. It's the only one of this color. Where did you find it?"

"I bought that piece when Mary and I went to Salem, Massachusetts about twenty years ago. We stayed at a lovely bed and breakfast and did a historical tour on the witches of New England. Wow, what an inquisition those women had."

"Another episode of life ruled by men, eh Sandy?"

"Yeah, there are a heap of male sins left in this world."

"Where did this one come from? It's so different from the others." I asked holding a brooch with a much larger cameo. It was translucent, tinted with topaz coloring. The ivory center was an outline of a female face and bosom, flowers in her hand.

"I found that at an estate sale in St. Paul. I remember the house was on Summit Avenue and filled with antiques. It's a bit heavy but a beautiful piece on a jacket or coat. This coral cameo ring came from that sale also."

After we made our selections, I said, "We'll treasure

these. The lovely ladies on the jewelry will remind us of the lovely lady we've fallen in love with."

Sandy smiled and said, "I'll miss seeing you every evening. Hearing about your work as a psychologist, Amy, made for interesting conversation. And, Vicki, your work at the church I know has meant a lot to Carol. You are such charming young women. Oh, to be in my thirties again. Enjoy, they are great years. But you need to start seeing the world. Travel, travel, travel."

"I think you've more than awakened our interest," replied Vicki. "Now, we need to take the first trip."

"Yes, sooner is better . . . come see me often."

"We will," Vicki replied. "You'll need help with all those thousand-piece puzzles."

"You can be sure I have more, and I'll take the cribbage board with me so we can continue our competition. Where do we stand? Amy, aren't you the leader?"

"Yep, I'm two games up."

Amy picked up the box of photos as she left and drove around the court to deliver it to Stan. We thought he might be the best caretaker of them for now.

Jan

My husband found me crying at the kitchen table with Sandy's Christmas letter in hand.

"What is it, Jan?" he asked, putting his hand on my shoulder.

"Can you believe this? How can this happen?' I mumbled as I handed him the letter. "Makes me sick." I got up and stood by the window, looking out at the patio where the three of us had enjoyed so many balmy California evenings.

Ours had always been a long-distance friendship, with

me living in California and Sandy in Minnesota. Our first telephone conversation was in 1977 when she made an inquiry about hiring our services to produce a TV ad for General Mills. Our friendship began that day even though our main topic was setting up a business arrangement. I've heard from so many of her friends that their friendships with her ignited in much the same way, during an initial contact by telephone.

Our home was her home, and her California trips often happened when we were away. We kidded her that she would have been successful as a professional house sitter. I smiled as I thought of her habit to journal her activities for us by leaving post-it notes on cupboards, the refrigerator, and the telephone stand. She stated her opinions of the restaurants she visited, new places for shopping, her treks in our car, and the wildlife visiting our backyard.

One of Bart's often-told stories is how Sandy interrupted his continuous fight to rid the backyard of ground squirrels whose sole purpose seemed to be chewing anything on our patio. During one of her spring visits, Sandy chronicled on her post-it notes, with an impish smile I'm sure, of her on-going friendship with Bart's little pests. "The two adult chipmunks really like chopped apples." "Saw two babies skittering around on the patio today." "Today lot's of babies, I counted twelve." "Babies prefer pear cut into small pieces." The topper was a small article left behind reporting that the one animal surviving the ice age was the chipmunk. She had attached a post-it: "doubt that you'll be able to overcome this type of staying power; maybe these are God's prized species." This became one of Bart's best stories.

"Hard to imagine that her last visit was really her last visit. She was my favorite house guest," said Bart. "Other than you, Jan, Sandy was one of few females whose company I enjoyed."

"I know. If I'd been the jealous type, my eyes would have glowed green for the many hours you two enjoyed together in conversation."

"You probably felt safe cause of her contempt for men."

"Well, I did notice she gave halos to few males. Lucky you were one of them. That was comforting."

"Just maybe she saw something special in me."

"I know you found something special in her."

"Yeah, I sure did. She provided such rich dialogue about books, religion, politics, and other cultures. So bright and well-read and held her own in any verbal exchange. And, we both know she doesn't suffer fools gladly. Such an authentic person and painless to be with."

"So true. I never felt any discomfort from her words, moods, or behavior."

"Well, except for the ground squirrels." And we both chuckled.

"I'll sure miss her Christmas box of homemade caramels."

"She never missed a year, even though sometimes the package arrived after Christmas."

"Yes, it was a grand holiday tradition." We silently read her letter again.

"Jan, why not call her and ask what we can do for her?"

"I will, Bart, but I'll need a few days to compose my feelings. I doubt Sandy would want me to call in a weepy mood."

And I'm glad I followed up on his suggestion. It was evident Sandy had a plan of action for which she needed friends.

"You could help a lot in January," were the words I

heard from her. "The house needs to be cleared for my move, and I have a thirty-year build up."

"I'd love to help and be there with you. How long do you think it will take?"

"There is so much to do. Imagine, thirty years and some stuff goes back farther than that. I thought with the help of a few close friends we might get it done in a couple of weeks. I'd really like you to stay three weeks. Can you?"

"That's iffy. For sure I can do two weeks. You name the day, I'll be there."

"Remember Mary who stopped by the house once when I was visiting you?"

"Vaguely. That was a number of years ago, but I recall you introduced her as one of your oldest friends and your traveling buddy, right?"

"Yeah. We shared a lot of life together. Well, she is coming from California also right after the New Year, and maybe the two of you could hook up at the airport and fly together."

"Good idea. Give me her tele number and we'll make it happen."

Two weeks later, Mary and I flew to Minneapolis. We luckily got adjoining seats and re-acquainted ourselves. After the amenities, we talked about Sandy and ALS.

"I have a friend who is nurse. She sure painted a dismal picture."

"Bart recalled he had a distant cousin with ALS. But, that was years ago and cross-country. We weren't first hand with it."

"There'll be a lot of pain and Sandy isn't good with pain. Plus, she hates pills."

"She has such a vibrant personality. Will it change?"

"Not sure how she'll handle this," Mary said. "Denial

isn't going to work this time. She might get cross. I was with her when she had back surgery in February. It's touchy when she's an invalid. She wants to be so damn independent."

"Yes, I believe that. She's always given the appearance of being in control. She's a proud person . . . makes her strong."

"I'm not exempt from being a control freak either . . . but a real marshmallow inside. I'm worried now about being in her presence, knowing she's going to die." Mary wiped her eyes. "She'll be upset if we cry."

"Probably good that we're there at the same time. Let's make a pact. If we feel ourselves giving away, let's go off to another part of the house, we could cover for each other."

"Let's try it," replied Mary. "And how about we split night duty."

"Are you a night owl?"

"No, I'm early to bed."

Stan met us at the airport and tried to prepare us for Sandy's condition. We walked into Sandy's townhouse and it seemed an affront to see her in a wheelchair. While she wasn't able to stand for greetings and hugs, the light in the eyes and smile was pure Sandy and left no doubt that she was delighted to see us. She had planned a social evening of lively laughter and talk, as was every evening that followed. The words, ALS, illness, and disease were never uttered.

The next day her working team, Mary, Stan, Jim, and myself began the dismantling of her household. Every item was brought to Sandy for her to see, hold, or read. Sandy decided whether the item was to be taken to Jones-Harrison, tossed, given away, sold, or put on a large tray by her chair for a second look. She sat in one of her Shaker chairs which Stan and Jim had made stationary to the floor, so she would not fall moving from it to the wheelchair. She sat with an elegant gold pillow at her back like a dowager queen, and we addressed her as Empress Sandy, making a game of bringing the items and, as lackeys should do, awaiting her decision. The fun of the charade gave relief to what could have been heart wrenching, a sadness which none of us wished to voice.

The devotion of her friends will remain with me. What an inspiration they were! There was a steady stream of people from morning until bedtime, somewhat like planned entertainment to keep her distracted from the depressive state of affairs. When she received a telephone call from some one inquiring about how she was doing, Sandy would pick up her calendar and ask, "Wouldn't you like to stop by? I have no one coming tomorrow afternoon." It was somewhat like recruiting people as she suggested a convenient time for a visit. Even though Mary and I were there all the time, she still needed the diversion of others. Mary thought it was because she didn't want to be alone with us . . . a tactic to hold off sharing her innermost feelings.

Except for one evening meal cooked by Mary, friends from General Mills or church brought food in every night. Full course meals served to us at the dining room table, dishes and kitchen cleaned before those angelic people left.

Being night people, Sandy and I had the late evenings to review the day's progress, laugh at the crazy antics we pulled off, discuss the people she had interviewed for the estate sale, praise the cooks, line up the next day: all general, upbeat, positive conversation. It was midnight when we'd say "bed time," and I had the intimacy of helping Sandy to ready herself for the night and tuck her into bed. I'd massage her legs until she grew drowsy.

My good night ritual was a kiss on her forehead and "I love you."

"Me too," she'd say. "Thanks for being here. You help make it easier."

Mary, who went to bed early, was the on-call person for the rest of the night. Sandy had a bell by her bed, with a noisy clang, to call her.

Sandy

My thoughts were on my two friends upstairs as I waited for sleep. Jan's warmth and gentleness, her soft grey eyes always clear, always calm, no edges, no conflicts. That aura surrounded her marriage and permeated her house. How I wish that my marriage could have replicated hers. And then vivacious, dynamic, energetic Mary always the stylish, petite, attractive brunette. I'm glad she keeps her color. She is noticeable and not shy. It was entertaining to watch the attention she gathered on our travels together. Our similarities evidenced in our stubbornness and inclination to be private. Mary has a straightforward, direct approach and I with snappish retorts. We could often be too quick with terse words and then tend to nurse our hurts in silence. Underneath, we are bonded by a fierce loyalty to each other that has never abated.

The next morning we started sorting through a thirty-year collection of household items. My friendly work team gathered around mid-morning. Jan served French toast for breakfast and kept the coffee brewing for those who came throughout the day. Stan and Jeannie helped, as work permitted, and we'd see Big Jim at the end of the day. He had the strong arms for lugging boxes up and down stairs. Mary Ann came late afternoon, often with dinner. They made a seat of honor for me by my bed in the living room, often giving dramatic performances as they brought every item to me for my decision. "Does the Empress wish to keep this?" "What are the Empress' wishes on this?" "Where did her holiness find this item?"

I couldn't transfer the making of these personal choices to others; I alone had to put closure to this part of my life. At first, I over-selected furnishings for the apartment, but with the group's decorating suggestions, I ended with a workable scheme.

Jeannie was titled the fashion coordinator and matched colors and accessories while I selected clothes for easy-on, easy-off dressing. Jewelry for each outfit was grouped into three compartmental jewelry boxes. She went through every piece of clothing with me, laughing when Stan modeled one of my more flamboyant outfits. He sashayed down the steps in my prized boutique white-on-black long dress. I said, "Go get the boa and camera." What a hoot!

"Why are you taking the heavy crystal glass bowl?" asked Mary.

"'Cause I love it. I bought it on my first trip to Europe with General Mills. The blending of red from the top down through orange in the middle and clear at the bottom made it a beauty."

"But it's so large and heavy. Are you that in love with it?" asked Stan.

"Don't you think it will be elegant holding candy chocolate kisses?" I replied.

"Yes, but do you need such a large bowl?"

"You bet. A lot of people will be with me, and we'll want chocolate comfort along the way."

"Like your signature piece, eh?" added Mary. "You are such a show-off, Sandy." I smiled and wrinkled my nose.

Finally, every item had a place: give-aways to charity,

junk to be trashed, leave-behinds for the on-site sale planned for February, or boxed for moving with me. Other items, like my new Saturn station wagon and a lot in Bisbee, Arizona, bought thirty some years ago when I was still married, needed buyers.

Jim offered to clean the house of all final debris left behind and Stan promised "he'd help carry Sandy's trash to the dumpster." I'd made arrangements for new carpet and fresh paint before the house went on the market. Again Jim offered his help to clean up after the workers and accepted, after a few polite refusals, my complete set of cobalt blue glassware as my gesture of appreciation. I felt Jim was a good home for the pieces. He so often admired the stemware whenever they graced one of our family meals. "I'll take good care of them," . . . he leaned over and kissed my cheek.

It seemed so unreal to disband my home in such a hurried fashion. Although it kept me preoccupied with things other than my condition, not preoccupied enough to keep myself from being short with those who'd come at my beck 'n call. I could hear my biting remarks such as "well, how would you know" or "don't push me on this" or "it's my business, not yours" and realized I expected my friends to overlook my verbal offenses. Mary would go quiet and invisible, a sign she was hurt. Bet she was ashamed of me. Jan seemed to ignore the remarks. Stan told me, "hush, don't be such a pill." Although it was because of my demands and their generosity that they were helping me, it was difficult to relate to them at times—ALS was happening to me, not to them. And, it was scary.

I feel strange, being detached from my personal surroundings. It seems as if memories are being trashed, pushed aside into hands of strangers. No one knows how hard this is. Guess I have to accept my life is over. Nothing to cling to except my friends; oh, how I'll need them with me . . . their faces, chatter, touch, laughter . . . otherwise I might sink into a black hole. Please forgive me my transgressions, for I know not what I do at times. I need you all so dreadfully—don't leave me.

Mary Ann

My role was being the food provider for the household workers. I brought in evening meals three to four times a week, mostly casserole dishes, in true Minnesota tradition. Besides, they were easier to prepare ahead of time since I had to be a full-time teacher during day hours.

"Where are the vegetables?" asked the California workers when I brought the third meal onto the table.

"In the main dish," I replied. "Are you looking for a particular one?"

"Your recipes are tasty, but I miss the fresh vegetables," said Mary.

"Guess, we aren't used to being in the Midwest during winter with no summer gardens," added Jan.

"Picky, picky," chirped Sandy. "Don't be too hard on the hand that feeds you."

I made sure that my following meals-on-wheels included fresh veggies and salad. I surely didn't want to offend Mary and Jan whom I'd just met.

Anything I do now to help Sandy would never be enough for the friend she'd become. She was old enough to be my mother and often attended to me like a daughter. Rather nice for me, since I'd been without my mother for many years. Like a parent would, she helped with the personal things. I moved into my new home in Maple Grove, not too many months ago, before the ALS diagnosis. Sandy packed and unpacked all my dishes, washing them in the new kitchen. Now I realize how much of an effort it must have been, all that standing without a complaint. She took a lot of time-outs, saying she'd wanted to rest her legs.

The last several years she helped me pack up teaching supplies at the end of a school year, counting and bagging all the little stuff, organizing the supply closet, making me more efficient. She came to my aid when Dad died on President's Day and I had to leave suddenly. She made my reservations, drove me to the airport on Sunday, lined up substitute teachers and showed up at the classroom on Monday morning to be sure the substitute was there. And the many nights I stayed late preparing class material, Sandy would show up with our favorite Culver hamburgers coupled with her offer of help. She knew my routine and inefficiencies so well, and without fanfare or censure, she'd put things in order so easily. What a friend, indeed! It will be like losing a mother a second time.

Sandy

The last day with my worker-friends ended with a lively dinner group of seven. Sadly, Jan had headed back to California earlier in the day and missed Mary's dinner efforts, for which we all declared she would not win the kitchen goddess award. When Big Jim, Patty, Marilyn, and Glyn arrived, they were put to work in the kitchen and setting the table. I'd asked Birdie to join us; her animated, bubbling personality would add merriment to the evening. Besides, Mary was heading back in a couple of days and I wanted someone with me till my move on the 22nd. Birdie would be the person.

After her divorce, Birdie had moved into the townhouse with me. That was almost thirty years ago, and in those early years, we worked closely in building both the women's sorority and Republican groups. Her network of friends was as wide as mine. We hadn't seen each other as often over the last ten years, but our friendship was glued by those earlier times.

"Hi, Birdie."

"Sounds like Sandy. Long time, no see."

"I know. Wondering if you have some free time this next week?"

"Sort of. What's up?"

"Remember how you always called me a pack rat. You used to chide me for saving every document for the sorority. Right?"

"Bet you are going to tell me that you still have all that stuff."

"Practically, Birdie, and I thought it would be a little bit of memory lane if you'd go through it with me."

"Gosh, Sandy, all that stuff is so old. Why not just trash 'em? Wouldn't that be easier?"

"Maybe, but I guess I want to visit a bit of the past. Wouldn't you enjoy doing it with me?"

"Being with you is good enough for me. But, sorting through old files doesn't sound too exciting. What would make them interesting now?"

"Maybe some old gossip. Maybe a few photos. Maybe some laughs."

"Promise to keep it to an hour or under?"

"We can try."

"How about next Tuesday?"

"Great choice. That's my last day at home. I move on the 22nd. You could stay for dinner and the night. I sure would love to have you here," I purred in my soft persuasive voice.

"Oh, Sandy, you're so obvious. What time do you want me to show up?"

"I'm dressed and ready for the day by ten. If you come then you can meet Ruth who starts my day every morning."

"I'll be there and I'll take care of lunch."

"How about staying the night? It would be sentimental for us to have the last night here. Remember our first night?"

"Yeah, we stayed up all night . . . bitching, moaning . . . then decided we were better than any male."

"We still are. Will you?"

"How can I refuse such an invitation? I'll check with you on Monday to see if there is anything else you'd want."

"Thanks, Birdie, you're a peach."

"Hey, let's not remind me that I'm plump."

"Well, aren't we both?"

Stan

Our last evening meal was good old-fashioned Dakota hash, more aptly known as a meal of leftovers. We washed it down with a couple of different wines remaining from the wine rack. Though I protested, the holiday dishes became mine that night. Sandy insisted on boxing them and sending them home with me. She fretted about clearing out the throwaway stuff and getting ready for the auction just ten days away. An opening for a volunteer.

"How about Saturday morning, Stan?" suggested Big Jim. "I'll bring my favorite baked egg dish to start the day."

"Gosh, I feel bad handing this mess off to you two," Sandy cooed.

"What's new?" I replied in jest. "You are great at running a project but your friends do the clean up."

"That's always been the way," added Birdie with a

chuckle. "It's Sandy at her best in the executive role, delegate the small stuff."

We all laughed and began a "remember when" round of stories, ending with Birdie's tale of cleaning out old files all day. Except for a few pictures, everything did end up in the trash.

"Boy, are you guys ever going to miss picking on me. Think I'll have to post a rule at Jones-Harrison—No Picking on Sandy."

"Oh, poor baby," we teased.

"Speaking of picking on people. How come you call Jim, Big Jim?" asked Birdie. "I'm rather sensitive to those words, after all one couldn't call me a dainty figure."

"Okay," I replied, "let's tell Birdie what we mean by *big*."

"A guy with a big heart—that's Jim." Sandy said, as she pointed a finger his way.

"A guy with a big laugh," added Glyn, imitating a deep belly-like laugh.

"A guy with a big grin," was my definition, as I bared my teeth in a wide smile.

"A big gut is what I've got," piped in Jim, rubbing his stomach.

"Whoa," said Mary Ann, "I think we can say Big Jim stands for a big personality. Cute and cuddly."

"Actually all those things are true," said Sandy, "and that's why we call him Big Jim. Plus, it highlights him from all the other Jims I know. I love cute and cuddly."

We went on to make the evening a casual, relaxed time: lots of jokes, tales and laughs along with a taste of Bailey's Irish Crème.

Sandy

At eleven everyone said good night, and I watched Stan walk across the lawn, with his brisk stride and a couple of playful hops, to his patio door. He blinked his porch light several times, our ritual for a final good night. I remembered how I snubbed him when he first made friendly, neighborly overtures. He'd moved into the townhouse complex twenty years ago and was the first single male in the circle. I'd pretend I didn't hear his greetings from across the common lawns or I'd go inside when I saw him come out his patio door. My cat didn't snub him, though. She'd head straight for his door whenever she got free of her leash, and I was to discover we were both cat lovers. Then, one of the neighbors invited him to our Saturday morning coffee gatherings and it became hard not to like Stan. He had a keen wit and amused us with his storytelling. He was an interior decorator and showered us with creative suggestions for our townhouses. He was a fellow native from North Dakota and never let me forget it. I had to overcome his being a Democrat.

"Why so quiet, Sandy?" asked Birdie, who had come back downstairs in her nightshirt.

"Just thinking about what I am saying goodbye to."

"You've been blessed with wonderful neighbors, haven't you?"

"None better than that guy who lives across the way."

"How I remember when you first started referring to Stan, and we teased you about having a male friend."

"Oh, you women were something again. Always looking for romance."

"Well, several of us did think maybe a love affair was in bloom."

"Yea, how unlikely and particularly with a man ten

years younger." I paused, before continuing, "There is a real love between us and it's like the love shared with my brother, who I cared for so deeply, or my nephew Larry, who has been like a son to me. Stan is as good as family."

"Kindred souls, aren't you? And the last of the original neighbors."

"Yep, over twenty years of memories reside here." Birdie stood quietly by my chair. I reached for her hand and silently crumbled inside.

It came so quickly, the final day at Golden Valley. Stan and Kolden, his Maine coon cat, were at the door with a pan of hot Pillsbury orange rolls for us, my all time favorite breakfast treat. It was a good start to a day that did not unfold easily or according to plan. The movers came in the early afternoon, well after the appointed hour that I had set with them, and took my bed and final items to Jones-Harrison. The medi-cab not showing up at all was the third misfire. Finally at 1:15 on January 22nd, it was farewell time, a very sad moment for myself and my neighbors in the Village. I called for Kolden, but being a cat, he sensed the sadness and had disappeared. Stan found him behind a chair and put him in my arms. All of this certainly did not fit to any kind of a plan that I'd held. It was heart wrenching, and I just let the tears flow. Kolden squirmed and pushed away.

I missed having Vicki or Amy with me the first night, their massage for my aching legs, and their personal touch in saying goodnight.

Oh, Mindy, how I wish you were here with me. It's been seven years since last I laid my hand on your soft furry tummy; a little rubbing and your purring was loving music. What comfort it would be to have you curled up by my side, such as we did for thirteen years. But you'd know death was approaching. You'd be restless and off your tuna.

The next jolt to my plans was the resistance from the staff to letting Ruth, even though a retired nurse, tend to my needs as she had done over the last two months. Ruth had come to the house each morning to help me shower, do my hair, dress and set up for the day, and now her qualifications were questioned. They said it was an insurance issue—liability. The end result was that Ruth would not be able to do the many things I had planned on, and I became the complainer I could be when things don't go my way.

Sandy

"Flowers for you," came a voice with a knock on the door.

Ruth walked over to receive a large box wrapped in lavender plastic. She carefully lifted the covering to reveal a gorgeous bouquet of my favorite colored roses, yellow and peach, standing tall in a white vase. The card read: *To brighten your new surroundings. See you tonight for dinner. Larry, Karen, and Myra.*

"What a lovely arrival, first thing on your first day."

"How sweet, just like them. All the family I have left," I told Ruth. "You met Larry over the holidays but not his sister, Karen or their cousin, Myra. The girls live in the Dakotas and are driving in today."

"You've mentioned Myra a number of times. She took care of your sister, her mother?"

"Yes . . . Joyce and Erwin were in Arizona, living the retirement life . . . Joyce suffered a massive stroke and normal lifestyle came to an end. She never really regained much use of her body. Her speech returned but just enough to carry on a semblance of conversation. I've always admired Myra for stepping forward and giving full-time care to her mother. They took Joyce back to North Dakota, and she cared for her in her home. I know it was a sacrifice, but she did it without hesitation."

"I had a friend who took care of her mother who had Alzheimer's. Evelyn was with her daily doing all the personal duties. It's not easy. Nor simple. It surely takes a big heart and loving spirit to give so much."

"Well, Myra has both. She's never been other than a beautiful daughter and niece all her years. I use to drive over to Bismarck as often as I could to give Myra and Erwin some relief."

We sat quiet. Then, "I find it strange that my sister and I were to live out the latter months of our lives without control of our bodies. Joyce was an invalid for five years. I doubt I'll be here that long." Quiet again.

"Are they staying for dinner?'

"Yes. They leave for Jamaica tomorrow, their first time going off on a trip together. I was supposed to go with them, but ended up left behind . . . oh well . . . how about we change the subject?"

"Have you made the arrangements in the dining room?"

"Yes, I mentioned it to the staff. They were going to reserve a table for five. Myra's friend, Judy, is traveling with them instead of me. But maybe we ought to go check with them, just to be sure."

A knock on the door and we heard again, "Flowers for you." A green plant with delicate purple flowers was followed by another mixed bouquet later in the day. My room was in bloom, even if I wasn't.

Larry

My initial worry about the quality of food faded with the delicate fish served in the dining room for our first meal. During the '80s when I was twenty-something, I had been a chef in a high-end Minneapolis restaurant to help with my college expenses and had learned the art of food preparation. Sandy was an excellent cook herself, so we both tend to be critical. Together, we had hosted many gourmet dinners. My taste buds this evening were not insulted by the flavors of the meal. Inwardly, I released a sigh of relief when I heard Sandy say, "I think we made the right choice."

"A stroke of luck for us, Karen."

"I like the ambiance and the food, and the residents look to be of sound minds, don't you think?"

"They are well dressed and seem congenial with each other," noted Myra. "The table behind you is enjoying a glass of wine."

Sandy eyed the room again. "Please note that at least seventy percent are women. I should find a few friends among them."

"Sandy, are you still going to discount the males?" scolded Karen.

"I've known enough males to last for me. I bet the age of the males in this room put them in the category of chauvinism. Ugh."

"You are the only other woman I know that has no time for men. In fact, you set a higher bar for men," said Myra.

"Did your other woman friend get ditched for a younger chick?"

"Now, now, remember my father was brother to your husband, and he did not desert my mother," said Myra.

"Remarkable, eh?"

"Hey," I waved my hand, "remember me? One of those males, you are talking about."

"Oh Larry, you know I hold you outside that no-account group."

As the tables were being cleared, Stan and Glyn walked into the dining room in time for a cup of coffee. As a surprise, Kolden was waiting outside. Their visit brought a perfect end to the first day and helped to launch a new beginning for Aunt Sandy. Back in her room, we imbibed in a cordial—her favorite Bailey's Irish Crème. To get all seven of us in a conversational circle, we rearranged furniture and put Sandy up front and center. With coaxing in soft cat talk, Sandy persuaded Kolden to leave his safe spot by the door and stretch out across her lap.

Stan looked us over and joked, "Well, here we are at her majesty's feet once again."

"But, where is my golden pillow?"

"For your feet or your butt?" quipped Karen.

"I could make a tiara out of the flowers," Glyn pointed to the roses.

"Perfect, a crown of thorns for having to put up with my court." Sandy laughed and threw her hands up.

"Lackeys. That's what we are."

As we were closing the evening of fun, Stan asked when the four of us would be back from Jamaica.

"In eight days," replied Myra.

"Wipe that frown and be of good cheer, Empress, for we will stay two days before heading back to Dakota," Karen said mimicking a frown.

"Can't I make a royal edict for more? Her majesty will want to hear of your travels. She may even have a few errands to do."

"Sandy, you'd want us to stay forever."

"Of course, why not?"

Sandy

Larry, Karen, and Myra had helped to fill my longing for children. They were the only nieces and nephews who'd made the effort since high school to remain close with me. Other nephews had ignored my gifts and overtures, and I'd not made contact in years. I don't ask about them and don't know where they even live. No one should be surprised why these three sitting here are the only heirs in my will.

Myra

I had this dream of traveling some day to an exotic place with Aunt Sandy. I'd envisioned being her travel companion to a foreign country, searching out the mystique, walking ancient ruins, and viewing masterpieces of art or wonders of the world. Some day, some day, I use to tell myself. First it was my job and not enough money. Then it was caring for Mom for five years and then Dad. So the dream was put off and put off. Now those "some days" have vanished.

There was a vacation in Florida many years ago, long before Mother's stroke. The folks rented a condo in Clearwater for a winter month, and Sandy took a week's vacation and a condo close to them. She invited me to join her. The four of us had so much fun on the Gulf. Sandy knew Florida quite well because, not surprisingly, she had a number of friends in that state also. She knew the boutiques that catered to the full-body figure (both of us), and we bought colorful sun wear and floppy hats. Her friends took us on their boat to quiet beaches where, like children, we sifted sand for seashells—Sandy selecting the unique and flawless for her collection, and I gathering shells just to have on my dresser at home. And no way can I forget the seafood platters at Bill's Shack on Maderia Beach.

Now here I am, free and ready to travel other countries and Sandy can't. I wanted to treat the four of us and found great bargain tickets last spring for Jamaica. At that time, Sandy's back surgery was over and her recuperation was projected to be normal. We expected the best. In the end, it didn't work out. Sadly, we know there is only one trip left for her to take, and it's a solo. It breaks my heart and shatters my dreams.

Karen

Now without Aunt Joyce and Sandy, there'll be no more of the annual all-girl weekends for Myra and me. The four of us use to meet once a year around holidays, either in Bismarck, Fargo, or Minneapolis, to celebrate our birthdays all at one time. Of course we did the shopping jaunts, the local shows—plays, festivals, and the splurging at top-star restaurants. But best was the time set aside for opening our presents. It was pure self-indulgence and pure enjoyment.

Sandy turned us into owlets for the night hours—four to six hours of sleep was the norm. But, what great times! Unforgettable!

Sandy

I busied myself with getting a letter out to friends announcing where to visit me and how to reach me by telephone. I wanted my mailbox stuffed and my calendar filled with names of visitors for days, times, and meals. Whenever friends called I asked, "When will you be by?" After dinner hours were the hardest. Watching television or writing letters was not my choice replacement for people. I could count on evening visits from Stan, Glyn, Mary Ann, Larry, Marilyn and, with time, I knew I'd persuade others. I also found out that animals could visit me and hoped Kolden would adopt my new place, although coon cats tend to be leery of new surroundings. And, Mary Ann could bring her dog, Hooper.

Larry

One evening, shortly after my return from Jamaica, Aunt Sandy asked me to stop by, saying, "I have some work I want you to do with me."

"What's up?" I asked as I entered the room holding out to her a small box of Godiva chocolates.

"Well, that will sweeten up the task. How's everything at work? Did the project move along while you were gone?"

"Yeah, it did." We chatted about what had been done during my absence and the new ideas I brought back with me. Then I repeated, "What's up?"

"Well, I thought this was a good night for you to come as no one else was going to be here. I want to talk about changes to my Living Will."

"Hum, okay. Are there a lot of them?"

"Not many. I just want the wording to be so clear that there'll be no hesitation later due to ambiguities. While you were gone I talked about my wishes with Stan and then had the attorney amend the document. It's in his folder in the desk. Look in the right hand slot."

"What changes did you make?" as I looked for the folder.

"I'd prefer you read all the pages, so that I can be sure you understand my directions."

"You mean right now?"

"Yeah, I mean right now."

Within an hour, I fully understood what Aunt Sandy wanted. She was adamant that no extraordinary measures be taken to maintain breathing or continue nourishment. If she herself hadn't accepted a breathing apparatus or feeding tube while she still had consciousness then they were not to be employed. It was clear that she wanted no artificial means for lengthening life once she had no movement of her body. She specifically wanted only friends by her side.

"But, Sandy, some of those procedures are for your comfort."

"Yes, but medication could also give me comfort if the end is near. I do not want to prolong the ordeal, okay?" Sandy said emphatically.

"Okay. I got it . . . but Sandy, you realize that a ventilator would help the lungs breathe in the later stages."

"Yes, I know, the doctors have explained that. And, I told them I don't want a tracheotomy performed. It won't affect the progression of the disease, only prolong life, which won't be much by then." Sandy pleaded, "Please be sure that doesn't happen."

"Okay, okay, I promise to see your wishes are followed." I sighed and lowered my head. "How many copies did the lawyer deliver?"

"Only two. Would you make three more copies? One for the clinic and another here in the desk for the home staff. Then, I told Stan I'd give him a copy also. The Medical Power of Attorney remains with you, but I thought Stan should be one-on-one with us. Don't you agree?"

"Yes, you rely on him a lot. I know he works issues here at the home and stays on top of what is being prescribed. I think he fights your battles, both here and at the clinic." She just quietly stared at me. "How about hospice? There's no mention of using hospice or outside services."

"We'll check that out down the line. A lot will occur between now and then. If my circle of friends lives up to their promise, I shouldn't need any hospice. I'm hoping also that we won't have to hire additional nursing assistance."

"Well, we'll see how much the staff can handle around the clock. But that's down the road also. I'll print these off tomorrow and drop them by on Wednesday when I pick up your laundry."

"Thanks, Larry, for Godiva, too. Yummy! Put them on the stand . . . I'll have one or two with the nightly news."

Mary Ann

I'm her scheduled visitor for Friday evenings, and this afternoon I was looking for short cuts as I drove from school to Cedar Avenue. I was late and trying to arrive in time for the five o'clock serving in the dining room. At noon I'd picked up the old movie *Shirley Valentine* and stopped at the liquor store for a bottle of Irish Crème. The British accent and London background of Shirley would open up conversation about our trip to Great Britain in the summer of 2001. And, the last half of the story was filmed in Greece, a country Sandy fancied as quite romantic.

We traveled to England with Pastor Carol and her husband, Neil, to attend Celtic spiritual studies in Durham. After that we paired off and went our separate ways. Sandy really took to the second part of our trip. In the late '70s I taught school in London for three years, which qualified me to be a guide as we toured the city by bus. I remember the day she fell to the pavement as she stepped from the bus. She was not quick to get up and accepted assistance with a great deal of embarrassment. We sat on a bench until her composure returned. She made light of the fall, as "being clumsy" and "such a klutz" but something else triggered within me. She fell too limply, unable to right herself, and I heard her remark "oh, not again." I'd heard her mention about a previous fall at a friend's house that surprised her, and I wondered if this type of accident was occurring more often than she wanted anyone to know.

But, we put the incident aside as we moved out of the city to the Isle of Marywelle for a quiet, introspective time in the Hebrides on the western coast of Scotland. Once again I witnessed Sandy's tactful, diplomatic, persuasive powers to change another's established mindset to one of her liking.

We'd chosen a lovely, old native-stone farmhouse now designed into a five-bedroom inn. It sat on a bluff, and our front room looked down over a wide green field whose border stretched along the sea. Patrick, the proprietor, was a hunk of a man . . . strong body and well over six feet. He looked like he belonged on a fishing boat. He was host for every meal and proudly served a sumptuous meal, both in taste and quantity.

In the evening, Patrick welcomed us with drinks and appetizers in the Sun Room, then dinner in the dining room before eight. The meal was more than ample: a tasty hearty soup, a very full plate for the main course, and desert with coffee. We'd be full to the gills half way through the meal. Patrick was obvious in showing his chagrin when he saw half-eaten meals taken back to the kitchen.

Sandy's fear of water—she couldn't swim—kept her on shore the day we went by small boat out to see the puffins. She had coffee with Patrick, working towards her scheme by giving him compliments on the food.

"Can't see that to be true when your plate and your friend's are only half eaten," said Patrick.

"It's too much for our stomachs to hold, but the food is

so delicious. Hope you notice we eat a bit of everything you serve us. Maybe do smaller portions?" I can see Sandy giving Patrick her most innocent, charming expression.

"Nope, can't do that. Customers might think they're not getting their money's worth. Not good for the reputation, you see."

"No, don't want to ruin that. How about my friend, Mary Ann, and I share the main course? In that way we'd eat all of the soup and dessert, and every plate would arrive clean back to the kitchen."

"Not sure that would be a good idea."

"Might you be willing to try it for a night or two?" I can hear Sandy asking a hesitating question.

"Can't just split the portions. Suppose I could serve a full entree to one place and an empty plate at the other. You'd have to split the portions."

"A great idea. Shall we try it? I promise we'll eat everything."

The next two nights went that way. A few other guests liked what they saw and asked for the same service. Patrick gave in and was obviously pleased that all the food was eaten. I chuckled how Sandy so adroitly worked issues with people, ending with her idea becoming their action. She was a master at steering things her way—I guess that borders on manipulation.

Stan

It was the 14th, Valentine's Day and the birth date of Sandy's dear friend, Patty, who I believe was the oldest in friendship and years. They'd started at General Mills about the same time and stayed on to their retirement. The birthday party was planned for tonight in the guest dining room; it's décor quite formal with a large dark mahogany table, which seated up to twelve. Sandy chose chicken for the menu. Marilyn, another friend from General Mills, was bringing a red and white wine to go with it. We men promised to buy tulips for the gals, and the women promised to bring chocolate for desert. I called at noon to check in.

"I'm looking for a valentine, Sandy. How about being mine?" She started crying when she recognized my voice.

"What's wrong? Has something happened to the plans for Patty's birthday dinner?" She just cried harder, unable to speak. A visitor picked up the telephone.

"Hi Stan, this is Deb. I've been here for the last hour trying to understand the situation. The staff informed Sandy before lunch that she'd have to move to skilled care."

"I hope she wasn't alone when they told her."

"She was."

"Damn 'em. I presume she's been crying and is distraught," I stated, knowing that Deb was being cautious in Sandy's presence.

"Yes, quite so."

"Have you confirmed this with the staff?"

"Yes. They've been in contact with the doctor's office to inform them of this change."

"Well, damn. Not friendly, eh? I wish these needs had been dealt with right up front. Another Sandy moment, in which she attempts to make life fit to what she wants versus what she needs. Let me speak to her."

"Hi, Stan. I don't get it. Why are they wanting me to be re-admitted to Jones-Harrison before I can be moved?"

"Well, I'm not a mind reader. I'll have to find out."

"Bet it's all because I have Ruth."

"Look Sandy, Glyn and I were planning to be with you tomorrow. I'll come early in the morning. For today refuse to move from your room. Meantime, get ready for the party tonight, and we'll deal with the other over the weekend."

"If you say so, Stan. What time will you be here this evening?"

"I promised Patty we'd pick her up at 4:30 and should be with you by five. Dry your eyes, repair your make-up, and put a smile on for Patty."

I knew I'd find a Sandy factor playing here—reality butting heads with her desires. Those times when, by choice, she will not process or comprehend the events at hand when they are not to her liking. She can't accept being an invalid. I've seen this increasingly become her behavior over the last six months. It's what I tag as "one of those Sandy moments," creating a false reality, pretending that she can organize life to suit her wishes. Her false reality doesn't stay undercover, and the ruse finally becomes public. She feigns ignorance and looks to others for resolution. I found the turning point for this one when I talked with Patty during our drive to Jones-Harrison.

Seems ALS made a significant move mid-week removing any ability for Sandy to stand on her own or take the two to three steps necessary to get from the wheelchair to the toilet seat. Ruth had remained Sandy's personal nurse, a fact they kept secret from the staff. Now Ruth was fearful that Sandy could fall without another aide at her side and finally had to say that she could no longer be her only caretaker. She told Sandy that at least two other people were needed to help her, and they should be from the Jones-Harrison staff. Ruth saw the reality of the situation and made today her last day. These disappointments seem to come as a surprise to Sandy and then she backs away, handing off the issue for one of us to take action. Her close friend, Mary, called from California on Saturday and

Sandy gave her only good news, never mentioning the turn of events of the past week. And, all within hearing of Glyn and myself who knew the real score. Only pleasant news to her friends seems to be her mantra and guiding principle. I've never seen Sandy in such deep denial.

With these insights I met with the staff to confirm that Sandy did need a sign-off from the doctor to move from her apartment to skilled care. What an interesting law that requires a doctor's approval and signature for even a move within a care facility. I shook my head as I heard their proposal of moving Sandy to a hospital emergency room so she could get a sign-off from any doctor there at that time. My response, "What a crock of poop!"

Patty

We were enjoying my birthday toasts, when Mary Ann paid notice to my jewelry. "Patty, that's an unusual cameo you are wearing."

"Yes, it is. Don't expect I'll see another person wearing a duplicate. Think it's one of a kind."

"Unusual to see a cameo made entirely of seashells, and such tiny ones," remarked Glyn. "Does it have a story to it?"

"Yes, it does, wouldn't you agree Sandy?"

"If I remember," Sandy smiled at me," I think it was our second winter vacation to Sanibel Island. We were strolling the town and, remember, it was a small boutique tucked away on a side street. We almost didn't stop cause you weren't in a shopping mood."

"For you who haven't heard, I'm more of a shopping companion than a shopper," I replied.

"When did you find it? Is it old? Was it a local artist?" asked Mary Ann.

Sandy continued the story. "Maybe twenty years ago, wouldn't you say, Patty? We started vacationing in Sanibel around 1980. Patty and I were always hunting out unusual seashells, in stores as well as the beaches. And when I saw this piece, I couldn't leave it in the store. It was so unique and a great addition to both my seashell and cameo collection."

"And, now it's Patty's?" asked Stan.

"Yes," I beamed, "it is my birthday present from Sandy. What a treasure for me."

Sandy

Well, didn't get my way this time. How disappointing! More independence lost. I'm not going to share a room. Maybe, a hunger strike would be convincing. Damn, what a nuisance this all is. But, I have no choice.

Within a few of weeks, we were packing again. I had to scale down my furnishings to one room and move to the nursing wing where most of the patients were in some stage of dementia. I was grateful that a private room became available and that I had the finances to afford it. My final location was on the third floor in the first room on the left, putting me fairly close to the nursing station and noisy foyer. A room at the far end of the wing would have been more quiet, but I wasn't going to fuss and give up the private room.

I'll have to work out different eating arrangements other than the dining room on this floor. I have to be with people who still have all their faculties; I'm barely being cordial in response to the inane words and rantings that I hear in the hallways. I need time to get use to them. Since I can maneuver the electric wheelchair easily, I'll suggest having my mid-day meal in the main dining room downstairs where I can be with my small group of newly made lady friends and push for having breakfast in the alcove where my puzzle table is set up. I'll think about evening meals, maybe a carry-in by friends or a tray from the kitchen. I'll get Stan and Marilyn working on this with me.

Stan says I'll just have to suck up and make the best of living in a nursing home and all the stuff life is dealing out to me. It's painful . . . all these adjustments, unwanted changes. I'm mad . . . so hard to settle into this. Goin' to have to let go and accept what comes. Damn it's hard! I'm going to have to give into the pills, too. It's either them or crying constantly which I detest more. Being weepy . . . feeling anxious . . . just an open door to self-pity. Stan warns I'd better improve my moods or my friends may not want to hang around. God, wouldn't that be awful. Damn it, bring on the anti-depressants!

It smarted when Patty told me I'm not too pleasant to be with, "Which is not like you," she said. And, I took to heart her following words. "We all are trying to live through this tragedy and your grief. You don't want to talk about it, but you're goin' to have to help us with a better frame of mind. Those pills you detest can help you and us."

And she closed with one of her favorite sayings, "After all, half a loaf is better than no loaf at all."

"That's what you've always said."

Patty

Dear Jan,

Sandy had been doing quite well in accepting her small living quarters until just this weekend. I know Stan e-mails you and Mary to keep you up to date, so you probably know we were out there Friday for dinner at Sandy's to celebrate a birthday that makes me older than all of you. She was naturally pretty upset by the fact they wanted to move her to the nursing home section on the following day. They needed doctor's approval for legal reasons but, of course, could not get it so late in the day on Friday. Sandy evidently checked her calls very late Friday night, and there was a message to inform her they were able to get approval.

Then, Stan, Glyn, Jim and Larry moved her on Saturday—many of her friends where there also. Everyone was pretty upset by the whole thing. Stan even talked about looking for another place.

Sandy did tell me she felt her arms were getting weaker, and just last Thursday, she was unable to stand at all. She now has a wheelchair, but it takes two people to get her into it. They do not have the staff or probably the training to handle her in the assisted living section. She is in the therapy area for now which is in the nursing home wing, awaiting a private room.

Hi to Bart and your great group of friends. I miss our trips to San Diego; glad Sandy and I had so many years with you at the house.

Love,

Pat

Sandy

I heard the knock on the door and turned around to see a pleasant looking woman, casually dressed in slacks, who seemed to be in her forty's.

"Hello. I imagine you might be Lisa who called yesterday."

"Yes, exactly right. Glad to meet you Sandy," she said as she walked towards me extending her hand. "As I explained the other day, I'm the staff nurse at ALS. My, this is a bright room, lots of sunlight. How do you like Jones-Harrison overall?"

"I haven't been here too long. I was in an apartment downstairs but had to move up to this room just last week."

"Something go wrong?"

"Not really, just that the staff here couldn't provide enough help for me."

"It's probably better to be near the nursing desk. I've visited another ALS patient who lives here. But not on this floor."

"Oh, if he is in a wheelchair, I think I've seen him in the dining room. Haven't really met him." I motioned to the chair, "Well, let's get acquainted."

"Have you lived long in Minneapolis?" Lisa asked.

"Since the '50s. How about you?"

"I grew up in a small town west of here. Came to the city for nursing school and stayed on. Took the position with ALS about six years ago. Do you happen to know about the chapter here in Minnesota?"

"No, this is all new to me and very much of a surprise. I wasn't prepared for this type of disease."

"It is overwhelming for anyone with ALS, that's why I like to make an early visit. We have so much we can help you with and also your family."

"I happen to be short on family, just one nephew here in the city and two nieces in the Dakota's. But I have a lot of friends and rely upon them."

"That's fortunate. Usually there are not enough caregivers. That's where we can help. In-home assistance, wheelchair, equipment, talking devices and we host a support group that meets . . ."

"Oh, I think not," I quickly interrupted. "My friends will be here with me."

"They are welcomed also and can come in the mobile van with you."

"Oh, I don't think so."

Just then, Patty walked in. "Here is one of my very best friends. Come join us, Patty. This is Lisa from ALS."

"I was introducing Sandy to the services of the Minnesota Chapter. Our offices are right here downtown, and we work closely with the ALS team at the clinic." Lisa turned from Patty to me, "Have you been there yet?"

"No, our appointment is in a couple of weeks. In fact, Patty will be with me."

Lisa mentioned we'd be meeting Jane at that time, a social worker and liaison between clinic, patient, and chapter. "Jane and I have known each other for a number of years. She is very dependable. I would imagine she is already working on the first item for you, an electric wheelchair."

"Well, I'll be happy to have wheels to get around."

"It's pretty simple to get the hang of it. Jane or one of her assistants will come with the delivery to instruct you." She paused, then, "Well, suppose you two might want to get on with your afternoon. I'll leave these brochures so you can see how much assistance we can give you. And, call me anytime, my card is clipped to the brochures. And, here's one for you too, Patty." Lisa turned to me, "Think about the support group, many attendees like the professional speakers. And, you're friends are welcome to join you."

"Where are you located downtown?" asked Patty.

"In the Union Office Plaza on Washington Street."

"Aaah, that's north of Hennepin, isn't it?"

"Yeah, the landmark we use is the Bijouterie. The Union is the four-story refurbished historical building right behind it."

"Oh, you mean the girlie business in the bright pink building?"

"Yesssss, one can't miss it," Lisa laughed. "You turn in on the north side of it and drive down into our parking lot."

"You all must be the butt of a lot of jokes."

"Got to admit there's a lot of kidding between offices about having a quickie lunch at the Bijou."

"You'd think the city could get that bright eyesore off of Washington Street, now that there're so many legit businesses in the warehouse district."

"That pink building has been there well before Union Plaza was re-furbished. Have to say their parking lot is never empty."

When Lisa was out the door, I said, "You can forget about the instructions, I am not joining a support group. Why would I want to share ALS with a group of strangers?"

"You wouldn't! You'd opt to go to the girlie show first."

"Well, anyway, I have a support group already."

"Nothing like friends, eh? Thank God, you are blessed with so many."

Deb

Sandy is getting careless about follow through or keeping people in the loop on her decisions. It's a new behavior not seen in her before. She makes a decision stopping a process or procedure and then grumbles or goes silent as if she's unaware of what happened. I wonder if it's part of the stress, disease, or depression. Stan now calls it the "Sandy Factor."

She was scheduled for a mammogram today (have to wonder why) and wanted me to accompany her in the van to the clinic. I arrived to find she had canceled the appointment (which made sense) but had told no one; just not like our Sandy of old. She was unhappy when I mentioned the inconvenience, and she wanted to blame the cancellation on the office (which wasn't true). I did a bit of scolding which upset her. I'll have to cut her some slack, I guess. I don't really know how this is all affecting her. She keeps her inner feelings so very private. I can only presume.

Mary Ann

"Mary Ann, are you coming by tomorrow night?" Sandy asked when I answered the phone. It was nine o'clock.

"Yes, I thought I'd bring a pizza for us. Hooper's coming also. Do you want a video?"

"No. We need to re-sort my wardrobe. I can't wear pants anymore, under or outer. Because of the way the lift works, I need a bare butt."

"Oh, no. We should have kept a few more skirts out of the clothes we gave away."

"Well, probably not. Think I'll need washable knits."

"Yeah, that makes sense."

"How about being my wardrobe coordinator and personal shopper?"

"We might ask Jeannie or Marilyn to help with the shopping. My schedule at the school is pretty heavy this next week."

"But you know my likes and dislikes better."

"Don't worry, we'll get it done."

Her voice changed from mother to child, "Oh, Mary Ann, my bowl is low on chocolate. Would you?"

"Well, we can't be without that comfort, can we? What kind?"

"Chocolate kisses."

Sandy

"Hello, Marilyn. I'm going to see you this week, aren't I?" I spoke into the phone.

"You bet. I thought maybe tomorrow at the end of the day. Or I can make it the next day. What's best?"

"Well, I don't have anyone for lunch on Thursday, the day after tomorrow."

"Works for me. I'll bring hamburgers and vanilla ice cream."

"Would you? We'd like that better than the lunch here."

"Any chance you have something special on the agenda?"

"Very perceptive for a ditzy blond, Marilyn. Thought we'd do a style show with you trying on the outfits made from silk I brought back from China."

"You mean the ones that Lorraine designed for you?"

"Yep, those two."

"Now, tell me why we are doing this."

"Can't wear slacks anymore. They're too cumbersome for the aides and me at toilet time. You always said you'd put your name on them."

"Well, that's 'cause they were so scrumptious. Is the beautiful quilted vest included?"

"Yes, they are all finally yours."

"Sandy, I'd love to have them. Are you sure? I'll pay for them."

"Absolutely not. They belong to you, Marilyn. Aren't you glad we're the same size?"

"Well, I guess that calls for a hot fudge malt instead of just plain ice cream."

"Either one suits me, just plan to stay as long as you can. There's not another visitor until early evening."

Patty

February 27th was Sandy's first visit with the ALS medical team at Hennepin Clinic. She'd asked Stan, Barb, Larry, Marilyn, and myself to go with her this first time. The doctor walked through the door and saw five of us sitting on one side of the room across from the patient in her wheelchair by his desk. He smiled and said, "Well, I'd better get my backups." He returned with four more people in medical attire. After introductions and explanations of the expertise of his team, he began asking questions to establish a time line for symptoms. Sandy held back the actual facts about the falls, the drop foot and inability to walk any distance. As we attempted to give the correct sequence Sandy would shake her head "no" or "oh, you guys," as if it had never happened. Stan said afterwards that he thought this was Sandy's way to deny that she had intentionally ignored those earlier symptoms.

It was a terrible heart-wrenching sentence that Dr. David laid upon us with his introductory remarks about ALS. He left nothing unsaid as he compassionately went from a description of the disease, on through its progress and affects upon the body, right down to the answer to Sandy's question. "How will I die?" I watched the shock flood across Sandy's face, and I felt helpless. We couldn't reach across the room to touch her, to hold her hand, to put an arm around her shoulder. The space between us was a huge chasm. If I felt fear, my God, what was she feeling? *I can hardly bear it. I musn't turn my eyes away; she needs our signs of love. Oh Sandy, how could this happen?*

Sandy

After four hours of meeting with the lead doctor, technicians, therapists, social worker, nutritionist, and pulmonary doctor, I had a thorough understanding of how they could help me through the months ahead. They'd be interfacing with Jones-Harrison staff to provide such things as range-of-motion exercises, wheelchair and braces, prescriptions, and any type of medical assistance an ALS patient requires. In time I would need a sleeping mask for oxygen and a feeding tube for nourishment and medication. When that time arrived, they would make the necessary arrangements with doctors and hospital. Their expertise with ALS and their compassionate manner gave me confidence in their team.

They prescribed medication to help reduce fatigue, ease muscle cramps, control spasticity, and reduce saliva and phlegm. Drugs were available to help with pain, depression, sleep disturbance, and constipation.

My prescriptions and dosage would be monitored to provide a good balance of comfort and avoid drug interactions. They didn't know how much I detested pills and would shun them as often as I could. Stan spoke up to tell them about my pill aversion to which they silently listened.

Finally, my greatest fear of choking or suffocating was given full attention. They discounted my preference for starving myself to death before the point when it would be difficult to swallow or breathe. Dr. David explained that starvation is not a painless death, and he gave assurances that I would be made comfortable with a breathing apparatus and medicine before my throat muscles lost their strength. Appointments were to be scheduled three months apart and the next one would be in May, but I was to call them at anytime with questions, needs or changes. Social Services would deliver a motorized wheelchair and provide instructions and training for its use; the therapist was the contact person for an array of devices available for people with disabilities. In time, I tried many of them.

I was forceful with my request to not prolong my life with extraordinary means. "Just help me through this with ease and comfort, as best you can, and I'll do the best I can. Right now I'm scared and somewhat depressed."

I left that visit feeling I had a competent, kind, big-hearted team who cared about me, as a patient and as an individual. They never let me down nor disquieted my initial confidence. I now had to put order into my life or of what remained of my life. I wanted to have a sense of normalcy. I wanted to enjoy the sociability and familiarity of my friends without their questions and concerns leading to gloom and doom. My disease and its outcome were not to be our focus of conversation.

Sandy, you must keep this from being maudlin and over-emotional. You can do it . . . you gotta do it . . . don't want to slide into the pit of self-pity. As the bumper sticker says, "Stuff Happens" and this is my stuff. You're going to have to make the best chocolate fudge you can out of this mess.

What proved to be the hardest was the process of acceptance I had to go through again and again. It was a non-ending succession of giving up, death stalking through my body. First the resignation to having no outs, no recourse to the sentence itself; next the relinquishing of control, giving my body over to the administrations of others; then would come involuntary submission to the loss of function—legs, arms, hands, breath, throat, voice. Anger, resistance, despair, sadness —are all emotions that emerge in the process of letting go of living. It's strange that my sister and I both came to the end in similar condition, a body to be cared for by others. I had compassion for her back then, and now I really know how bad it can be. It's detestable!

Peggy

I called Sandy to tell her that I'd re-arranged my schedule to open up Wednesday afternoons for weekly visits, at least for the next couple of months. I was relieved when she said, "That fits into my calendar well." I told her she could expect me around two o'clock.

"Come earlier if you can and stay as long as you can. Hey, I got a nice card and note from Jim Ramstad last week. Have you seen him recently?"

"No, though I understand he was in town for a Republican fundraiser, but Paul and I had to be down in Rochester that day. It's the second time I've missed him this year. Though you know I've really dropped out of the political arena since I left the Legislature."

"I know. You surprised a lot of us. Hear you do a lot of community work in the suburban school districts."

"Yeah, guess we do have a few years to catch up on . . . it'll be good to see you again."

"Maybe we'll find a political story or two," she chuckled.

Our friendship was grounded in politics. She walked into the beginning of my political life with incredible resources. A Rolodex of names that never quit, a stable of women friends who'd answer a call to do whatever task was at hand to be done, although not all of the women were enmeshed in politics as strongly as Sandy. But, they came when she called. She brought to the table boxes of campaign literature collected over the years from which we garnered ideas for such things as direct mail, brochures, and fundraising events. And she had organizational skills that could knock your socks off. She was awesome as a campaign manager and treasurer. Many fellow Republicans told me how fortunate I was to have Sandy—think they were a bit envious.

Another Republican who had received the initial party endorsement, but then preferred to run for Congress instead of the State Legislature, referred her name to me. He recommended Sandy saying, "She is one of the best you can get" even though she had refused to work as his campaign manager. The reason for a "No" to him and a "Yes" to me hinged on our stance on pro-choice. I was, he wasn't.

Sandy was strongly opinionated, and her political stances were rock-solid and uncompromising. She was no knee-jerk Republican, but she respected the policy of less government in the affairs of state and individuals. Over time, I believe she truly became fed up with the conservative wing of the Republican party and relentlessly worked to counteract the right-wing influences in the caucuses. I saw her as moderate to liberal; open minded and tolerant of social issues; fiscally responsible but finally suspect of the numerous government social programs and their administration.

Her hard-working energies matched mine, and we formed a model for campaigns that served me well for six elections. I did the fund raising; she ran the campaign. I shall always admire her astonishing ability to make things happen through others. People stepped up to work on tasks just because of Sandy. She was persuasive and never expected, nor accepted, less than a positive response to her requests for help.

And, who will forget her trademark—homemade Christmas rosettes and caramels!

Ann

How often I've told of my political faux pas made in Sandy's presence and the tongue lashing which ensued. Patsy, Kathy, and Sandy were sitting around my dinner table when I casually said I'd be giving my vote to the Democratic presidential candidate. You would've thought I'd jabbed a tight fist into Sandy's jaw. She scowled, raised her back into a rigid spine, and shot a loathsome glare at me.

"Are you out of your mind?"

It was the Bush/Clinton contest of 1991. "I just don't think Bush portrays a strong leadership presence."

"You're going to cast your vote for a liberal yuppie?"

"Well, he's been a state governor."

Wow, we received a thirty-minute passionate lecture on Bush's background and the harm in not electing a Republican.

"Sandy, for crying out loud, I am only one vote."

"And, it belongs to Bush. You're a registered Republican."

She checked on me right up to the election. Yes, I remained loyal and voted for Bush.

At the same time, Sandy was very concerned with the concentration of the religious right wing playing out in the caucuses. She urged us to get involved, "If you don't, you won't like what you'll see ten to fifteen years down the road." How true her warning proved to be.

E-Mail from Stan

Another tough moment for Sandy today. A significant reality check. There was one other ALS resident at the Home, and he died this week. He was only fifty years old and had been in the home for maybe eleven months. Sandy had seen him in the dining room yesterday, but today his table held flowers and his picture—he was fine at dinner and gone the next morning. She immediately assumed that he had choked during the night and remarked, "He didn't even make it a year." Not much to say to a moment like that.

Glyn, Jim and I stayed the evening to work on the puzzle she set up in the alcove off the main hall. I notice how her hand and finger control is deteriorating. She even commented that she thought her puzzle days were limited—another pleasure to come to an end. She just can't pick up and manipulate the pieces. However, she still can shuffle and deal cards and is cagey in her playing. She loves winning over all us males!

Sadly, animals are not allowed in the nursing wing, so Kolden no longer can visit Sandy. He may be glad but Sandy is not. She'll probably grouch about it to the staff. Maybe I could bring Kolden to the patio when warm weather arrives.

Patty

This was a congenial day, although that was true for most of the times we were together. It was Sunday, one of my days for visiting. I came mid-morning, after Mass. Sandy and I shared different views about religious worship and political affiliation. We've had a life-long, friendly, back-and-forth ribbing between us.

She: "Catholicism restricts the individual."

Me: "Catholics are not the Republican party."

She: "Catholic religion is so exclusive."

Me: "Yeah, not like your new-age, free-love church."

She: "So heavy in ritual."

Me: "Bet that doesn't interfere with Catholic prayers; they get answered as well as yours."

I know she'd once been a member of the Methodist church with her husband and felt abandoned when the congregation turned their back on her at the time of the divorce. So much for traditional religion, even though over the years, the Methodist minister kept in contact with Sandy.

We'd read and mull over the Sunday paper, often moaning about the upcoming events in Minneapolis that we wouldn't be attending. She'd have coffee brought up from the kitchen to go with the muffins I'd bring. After finishing the weekly crossword puzzle, I'd let Sandy choose the agenda for the day, fitting to what she'd like to do. Sometimes it was the current jig-saw puzzle, or maybe we'd go down to the office area to send e-mails to Jan and Mary, or when weather permitted we'd be out on the patio taking in the sun. We didn't watch much TV together, rather we preferred reading books or current magazines, which would kindle provocative conversation between us. We enjoyed the bantering in which we often engaged. It was our style and a type of entertainment when we were together. It had always been that way with us. We called ourselves "the jolly twosome."

I stayed through the day, having lunch with her in the dining room, until visitors came in late afternoon or early evening. Invariably, she'd say, "You don't have to leave." She'd act miffed, attempting to lay a bit of guilt to get me to stay longer, and always trying to extract a promise I'd be back before the next Sunday visit. Sandy did not like being alone; in fact, it seemed she could not be alone—an obvious trait that appeared after the divorce and became more so with ALS.

Except for our first flood of tears, we never broke down again, although we often had watery eyes. The subject of dying or death was not a part of conversation, a preference, I believe, for both of us. As close as we'd been, Sandy never shared her fear; one only saw it in her face or her behavior. The subject was off limits, as if to go there, one would cry which to her might be a sign of weakness or giving into the circumstances. Her real feelings about her physical condition were kept under private wrap.

Sandy

Patty and I have a lot of history together, going back to our early days at General Mills. While we had different interests (she is one friend who successfully escaped my pressures to join political and sorority groups), we had respect for the differences and plenty of good times to override them. She is a devoted friend, and I love her dearly.

Patty has always been petite and worn slacks much of the time away from work; it gave her a Katherine Hepburn flair. Most of us thought Patty could have been a comedy actress. She could lighten up any situation with a ready quip, a humorous retort, or a wise Irish saying. My favorite was: *Loyalty not properly learned is an enemy.* She'd had serious health issues in recent years, and I was scared we'd lose her. But it will be me leaving her behind.

Time seemed to be of the essence, and while I still had vitality and a modicum of control, I got on with settling my affairs right down to planning the memorial services. And Pastor Carol and Mary Ann, the person with whom I had co-chaired the BeFrienders program at church, stepped up to the task with me. First, Carol brought me the church's Book of Worship to study and to help me plan what I wanted in the services. She reviewed the order of readings and music the book set forth and pointed out that each had alternates, which should offer plenty of choices.

Carol and Mary Ann came the following week, spending a morning to help me finalize church arrangements. I had opted for cremation, as I've always been adverse to an open casket. Where the ashes would finally rest remained undecided. It either would be in North Dakota with family or in Minneapolis—Lakewood where my baby daughter is buried. I was uncertain and when it is all said and done, "what difference does it make?"

Interesting that I feel I must orchestrate my final ceremony. Some will wonder why it was necessary, but it is. I want my life, no matter what the count of months remaining, to be according to what I want. Guess I've always been this way—having control. And, look at what my final months will be—no control . . . the ironies of life.

"I appreciate you being here with me. Trust this won't take too long. I went through the book, Carol . . . just want to get this over with."

"I know it's hard, Sandy," replied Carol, "but let's make it right. A memorial can be a beautiful gift to leave with friends and family."

The three of us talked first about our favorite readings, then choices of prayer and even sang a few of the proposed hymns.

"The music is easy," I said. "I love 'How Great Thou Art,' particularly sung by a baritone. I called the choir director David and asked if his son-in-law, Greg who has such a gorgeous voice, would sing." I paused and they nodded in agreement, "Good choice."

"David thought Greg would be pleased to do so but said I'd better have a back up. Seems he travels a lot and could be gone. Is there anyone else in the church who has a baritone voice that we've not heard?"

"Why not let me work on this with the choir, Sandy?" offered Mary Ann. "Maybe we can find another baritone for you, even if it's outside the congregation."

"I'm choosing to open with the choir singing 'Hymn of Promise.' The words are appealing. I always have the image of a butterfly coming out of a cocoon. It's a hopeful message, don't you think?"

"It's a nice choice," Mary Ann agreed.

"That could be followed with a greeting and a prayer you'd like to read, Carol."

"Okay, if that's what you want," Carol nodded. "And then we follow with 'How Great Thou Art?'"

"Yes, and of course, you know what I'd pick for the scripture reading."

"It would have to be Psalm 139, Verses 1-12. Really nice lead into the meditation."

"Oh right, that Psalm is your favorite. Someone particular to read it?" inquired Mary Ann.

"Yes and no. I want a person of the congregation. Maybe Linda. Guess I'll have to check with her."

Like perfect timing, a nurse came in with my morning pills, breaking up the serious atmosphere. Mary Ann went to the kitchen to see what was available; she came back with coffee and cookies. Carol finally guided us back to the services, the segment for personal messages.

"Usually, friends give their remembrances next. How

many do you think would be speaking?" asked Carol. "For the many friends you have, we could be there all day."

"And night," added Mary Ann. "Perfect for the night owl, eh? Wonder how many could go the distance."

"You might be surprised. I've trained them well."

"Well, I know I wouldn't last that long," quipped Carole. "Come on now, let's move on or we'll be here all night."

"Okay," Mary Ann started, "Sandy asked if I'd do the words of remembrance and looking at this outline, I'd presume I'd open it to anyone who also would want to step forth to say words of remembrance."

"I certainly wouldn't want a trail of people," I interjected. "I think fewer words are better."

"You know, it isn't necessary to open it up at all," replied Carol.

"Wait a minute. For sure, I want to ask Mary, Stan, and Patty . . . three at least and maybe four to speak for me." With a bit of hesitation I had to add, "Mary may not come from California and would be reluctant to read anyway. She doesn't do emotional situations well and would hate to break down in front of a crowd. The same is also sort of true of Patty. It may be just Stan and Mary Ann, and that's probably enough. And of course, Carol, as pastor you'd be doing the prayer of thanksgiving and intercession."

"Yes, of course. But, what about your bio—your personal history that becomes the words of remembrance? Who's your reader? Are you working on that? Your nephew . . . or a niece?"

"No, they preferred to keep their participation open. It'll be Mary Ann." I gave her my sweetest smile. "Isn't it?"

"It would be an honor, darling Sandy. Are you writing it or me?"

"Let's say both of us. I've been thinking about the piece for the newspaper also, which led to donations. I've always disliked seeing a funeral overwhelmed with flowers. It seemed to me a smell of falseness, like an atonement for things left undone. I'd like to keep flowers to a minimum. Maybe I'll give you an order, Mary Ann, for a few of my favorites and request donations in lieu of flowers."

"Bet it will be the Humane Society," she said.

"Yeah, for all those dear kitties who are looking for homes. Guess, I'd want ALS also, for their research and aid to patients."

"Do you mean to use the same bio for church reading and the newspaper?" asked Mary Ann.

"Not sure. We'll work on the bio together."

"You mean Mary Ann and you or the three of us?" asked Carol.

"No, I think we could do it, right?" as I sent Mary Ann a pleading glance. "Particularly since you're the one who will be reading it."

True to being a loyal friend, she replied, "Maybe we could do it during spring vacation."

"Yeah, that ought to fill an hour for us. If the weather is nice, we could work in the patio, and you could bring Hooper."

"I've always wondered," Carol chimed in, "why you tolerate Hooper after I've heard you put dogs in the same view as men."

Mary Anne quickly answered with, "Oooh, I think Sandy knew a friendship with me had to also include a friendship with dogs. Guess I'm lucky she didn't discount me because of Hooper."

"It's true, I never thought I'd hold a dog on my lap, but it's easy when we drive up to Mary Ann's cabin. Hooper sits quietly and let's me pet him," I told Carol. "Hooper and I have found our base; it's playing 'toss the ball and fetch.' Guess old dogs can change their opinions, eh?"

"It didn't hurt too much, did it? Not much different than accepting a few Democrats as friends," Mary Ann said with a broad grin. "Otherwise, we would have missed all those summer days and mosquitoes at the cabin."

"That's for sure. Wonder who will be washing windows with you this summer? I was one of those people who did do windows, you know. Well, better get back to the planning." I looked at my notes and continued, "The bio would come after 'Beautiful Savior' and then the book indicates the Affirmation of Faith is next, read in unison."

"Yes, that works nicely," said Carol. "Than another song?"

"I'd like to insert the music sheet of 'On Eagle's Wings' into the printed program. It's a lovely piece for everyone to sing." And so, we continued selecting the rest of the music ending with Bach's 'Come Sweet Death.' We sat still for a few moments, glad the task was done.

"Let's break open the box of See's chocolate . . . just received from California yesterday."

As Mary Ann decided whether she'd choose a caramel or a cream, she brought up the question about a menu for lunch after the services.

"I thought about using an outside caterer."

"Well, Sandy," Carol interjected, "I suspect that the people from the church who brought you meals in November, December and January would want to prepare the luncheon."

"Right," said Mary Ann. "You know we've served food after services in the past, and I think your friends at church would want to prepare your menu."

"It just seems they've done so much already."

"Well isn't that why we're all proud of our church? Let's talk with Lynne about this," suggested Mary Ann. "She the coordinator."

"I suppose you'll want a chocolate desert?" Carol said light heartedly.

"Of course. And I thought we'd place bowls of chocolate kisses throughout the church also. Could you tolerate that Pastor?"

"Well, that will be different and certainly not listed in the *Book of Worship* but whatever you wish, Sandy," Carol replied with a shake of her head and a half smile. "Will we have to bless 'em?"

And so it went, item by item through plans for the entire service, arriving at an acceptable outline. Others could decide later about where to place the easels of pictures I had yet to sort and select. The morning took its toll on us. Carol and Mary Ann were pressed to accommodate my wishes, and we were talking about my good-bye to living. It was emotional with several time-outs for a few tears patched over with idle chatter, then we'd pass the bowl of chocolate kisses.

Gert

I admired Sandy's bottomless well of unselfish service she gave to the church. She seemed to be one who really had it all together, whatever it is. She was efficient, could make things happen and be so, so convincing. She and Mary Ann started, and co-chaired for several years, the BeFrienders Club, a one-on-one support group within the church. They gave their first presentation one Sunday morning and set up recruitment following the services. I listened as they spoke about the program, which promoted the befriending of a parishioner by another. One prerequisite was training, and then you would be matched with someone needing a friend in some area of their life. Sandy handled the presentation and sign up, and Mary Ann would do the training.

I didn't plan to sign on to the program and went in after the presentation prepared to give Sandy my "no" but came out a BeFriender. She had an uncanny natural ability to turn a "no" into a "yes" before you'd hardly even said the word. I chuckle about it to this day.

Sandy

Gert stopped by today bringing a couple of twigs from a plant in her yard known as a burning bush. Spring buds of a bright burgundy red were on the twigs, and when I held them horizontally in the sunlight, they did look like bright flames. We laid them amongst my flowers on the windowsill to catch the morning sunlight.

She also brought us authentic Greek salads for lunch with extra portions of black olives (I loved olives of any kind), along with chocolate and vanilla ice cream for dessert.

"Did you make the salads this time?" I asked.

"No, I ordered them from Christo's. It was a toss up between them or It's Greek To Me."

"I wish I could talk the kitchen chef here to make a salad like this. Their version is short on feta cheese and real Greek olives."

"I brought us silverware also, plastic forks hardly go with a gourmet salad."

"You are first-class, Gert. Why don't you stay the evening? Our friends Louiva and Jim are coming by. That makes a foursome for cards."

Gert

Sandy and I joined the church about the same time and were the same age, I suspected. Although I'd never talked with her directly, I'd heard from others that she traveled a lot. After several months, she and I happened to sit next to each other at one of the services.

"I understand you're a world traveler. Do you have any new trips planned?" I asked her, as a way to open a conversation.

"Yes, in fact, I do. I'm starting to think about Egypt in November and have just made inquiries of a travel agent two days ago."

"Ah, that's a place I too have wanted to visit."

"Well, would you like to join me?" was her quick reply.

The surprise response took me back a bit before I said apologetically, "I'd have to invite a friend who has my promise we'd make the trip."

"That would be fine with me. I may invite a friend also."

Sandy followed up by sending brochures within the week. My friend, Marian asked if Sandy was religiously rigid. While I perceived Sandy to be deeply devoted to the church, I also sensed that she'd be right there when good times were coming on. We all met for dinner soon after and found we could share drinks, humor, and congeniality. The trip to Egypt was on its way to becoming reality and so was a friendship.

Sandy

I focused on giving my room the atmosphere of a friendly home, my space where pleasantries were the norm. Friends aided and supported me in keeping a cordial, social atmosphere. Underneath, we all knew what the final score was, and I deemed we need not speak of it. Making the present moments the best ones was paramount. As spring weather approached, our visiting hours often were in the garden courtyard where flowers and bushes were blooming. I'd always been a lover of sunshine, and it was exquisite to feel its warmth on my face, arms, and legs—a momentary respite when life seemed sane and ordinary.

My days settled into the typical routine of a nursing home, a defined schedule for meals, baths, therapy, and medicines. Most of the aides and I became good friends. We talked a lot about their families, aspirations, and life in America, as most of them were natives of African countries. They learned my needs and engaged in selecting my dress and jewelry most days. We discovered where our humor met and laughed at our private jokes.

Charles always entered the room with a long face and his answer to my question of "Why the long face?" was, "I miss my family. They are still across the ocean, and it will be a long time before I see them."

"Who are your family, Charles?"

"My mother, sister, brother, wife and twin boys."

"Having a long face won't make them cheerful. Why don't you bring in their pictures for me to see? I'd get to know about them, and we'd give them a smile each day."

Emile was the opposite. I could hear his humming as he approached the doorway and then a cheery, "How's my Miss Sandy today?" He liked to come in early so he could help me select my dress for the day. I sensed he enjoyed searching through the jewelry boxes for the pieces I'd described. He'd carefully put earrings in my pierced ears and a brooch on the shoulder of my dress. He'd step back, nod his head and say: "You look lovely, Miss Sandy. All ready for breakfast and visitors."

Sensa always stopped in before and at the end of her shift, wanting to know how I felt. "Was I better?" "Where did I hurt?" "Had I eaten my food?" I always held forth the bowl of chocolate kisses for she was as much a victim of chocolate as I. Sensa was just a slip of a gal and needed help when moving my body in the lift. She had a gentle presence, and her solicitous concern was continuous and touching.

The chink in the set-up was the turnover of employees, and it became a weekly chore to orient and train at least one new aide to my disabilities. I certainly could understand that a daily routine of lifting people, giving baths, wiping butts, being the strength of legs and arms for a human takes its toll. The employee can transfer or leave, the patient cannot. So, the ever-changing work staff can have a discouraging affect.

Good old Stan was my mainstay when it came to interfacing with the Jones-Harrison staff. He attended the regular meetings where current issues were evaluated with nurses, dietitians, and social worker working out the best course of actions going forward. Stan kept the notes and followed-up in my behalf when changes needed to be made. Over time another friend, Barb, joined Stan in being proxies on my behalf, and they pulled in the female chaplain to be an effective advocate when needed. The thought of how awful it must be for those who have neither family nor friends to fulfill such roles was a sour one. I could count blessings even in these grimmest of circumstances. Life continues to have grace, bringing joys and gifts through the many beautiful people in my life. For this, I give thanks.

Stan

We had a standing Friday morning breakfast date. I arrived early to comb her hair, pick out a set of jewelry for her dress of the day, and put the earrings into her pierced ear lobes. The staff brought a tray for me, and we'd eat breakfast in the lounge area. We engaged in the usual tiff about taking pills, as Sandy decided which ones she'd take, the rest just disappeared into the trash bag hooked to the side of her wheelchair.

"There'll come a time when you might be sorry for trashing those pills," I'd say in a stern voice.

"I doubt it. I can always get more from where these came from if I change my mind."

"Sandy, you are so set against medication. Stubborn, is more like it."

"Yep, that's the way it is." *End of conversation.*

One Friday morning, we broached what might be in the remembrance she'd asked me to prepare for memorial services.

"Well, Sandy, what shall we say about you?" I mused. "I have several fantastic ideas myself. How irreverent may I be?"

"Ha, as if I could keep you from the theatrical part of you."

"I'd like to speak to the mutual ties we had, like North Dakota, cats, gourmet dinners, our woes and joys. Of course, all done in my 'no holding back' style."

"Please, oh please, don't include one of those old worn-out North Dakota jokes."

"You mean like this one? In Dakota, if you have an unpleasant neighbor, chances are she does too." We shook our heads at that old one. "Or this one? It's true Dakota farmers eat peas with honey; not for the taste but because they stick better to the knife."

Sandy laughed. "I've probably told you about a thrasher who helped on Grandpa's farm . . . he ate everything with his knife. I would hang around the table just to watch him until Grandma shooed me away."

"We could use some of the old sayings our Minnesota friends laid on us. Remember this one? A North Dakotan is so narrow minded, their ears rub together."

"Yeah, another one was, in North Dakota lots of people play dumb. Unfortunately, many are not playing."

"Of course, I could put in some of your favorite sayings about men."

"Oh no, we could forgo them, don't you think?" Sandy grimaced.

"You mean you wouldn't want the congregation to hear, 'He's not entirely useless, he can serve as a horrible example.'"

"I thought one of my best was, 'Good men are as few as trees in North Dakota.'"

"Or your classic, 'Some of the best boy scouts are girls.'"

By this time we'd laughed so loud, people had stopped to listen. One of those wonderful, lively, fun moments that were still possible.

Patty

My birthday in February and now Stan's in May. I hosted the dinner, making arrangements through Sandy for the private dining room. Big Jim brought the wine, Stan thought of Manhattans, and I made a lemon pie for dessert. I'd bought little monkeys swinging from a palm tree for party favors and a small flowering plant for the centerpiece tonight and Stan's patio tomorrow. We were in a festive mood, behaving like youngsters, or maybe like silly monkeys swinging on a good time.

Stan was quick to remind Jim that smart remarks about being fifty were not in order. "After all," he reminded, "you just had your fiftieth in December and should remember the sensitivity about turning the corner of age."

We all kidded Glyn about being too young to understand the importance of the half-century mark. And, I reminded everyone that they had a way to go to catch up with me, after all I was the oldest. Sandy was quiet as usual about her age, as if we all didn't know she was 73.

Sandy wore a new skirt that Carol had made for her. Because she always wore solid colors, we ribbed her about the bold print pattern. When I told her she looked great and should wear splashy prints more often, she wrinkled her face into that Sandy look of disapproval, "You people!"

I noticed Glyn looking at the diamond ring on Sandy's hand and he finally asked: "Wow, where did that rock come from? I never saw you wear it before."

"Guess cause I don't wear it often."

"Was it a secret lover?" No response from Sandy.

"Own up, Sandy," I said, "You didn't buy that."

"Who was it?" asked Jim.

"Oh, someone from years ago," replied Sandy. It was a hurdle for her to admit that a man gave her the ring.

"If my memory serves me correctly," I chimed in, "a little bird told me that it was a jewelry salesman you dated for awhile?"

"That little bird must have been a stool pigeon," came Sandy's quick reply.

I just had to add, "A secret is not a secret if it's known by more than one person."

"Come on, Sandy, own up. Give us the scoop," chided Jim.

"He tried . . . and lost . . . and was the last man I dated."

"Poor fellow, he probably never knew that you never trusted a man again after your divorce," I said. With that I could sense Sandy was ready to change the subject.

Although Stan wasn't. "Here's the world's shortest fairy tale. Once upon a time a guy asked a girl, 'Will you marry me?' She said 'No' and he and she lived happily ever after."

"Bingo!" I yelled.

Sandy raised her hand, "I second that."

"Stan, bet you made that up," laughed Mary Ann. "It's perfect."

Stan gave us his impish grin and rolled his eyes.

"I thought I'd have the diamonds made into ear studs for all you good guys in my life," Sandy said with a teasing smile. "There's you three, and Bart, and the other Jim, Marge's husband. All you have to do is get your ears pierced."

"Sure, brand us as Sandy's good scouts. No thank you," said Stan.

"I'll be satisfied if I could take all the monkeys home," said Jim. When we looked at him with raised eyebrows, he said his mother loved monkeys, in fact collected them.

Glyn sighed. "Thanks, Jim, for changing the subject."

Later when it came to singing the birthday song and opening cards, Stan asked Jim to read his birthday greetings from Sandy. I'm sure to save them both from tears.

A pretty birthday card I couldn't get out to buy,
Even for the birthday of my very favorite guy.

So I had to write my own rhyme,
Saying "violets are blue"
To tell you on this birthday that I Love You!

Overall, it was a cheerful, giddy evening. The antidepressant medication had leveled out Sandy's mood swings and she was a joy to be with again, every time.

Vicki and Amy

"Hi, Sandy. Oh, you're alone. Usually you have a room full of people."

"Sadly, my evening visitors couldn't make it today. You must have ESP to know that I needed company."

"Well, here we are, just for you. Anything special going on?"

With that Sandy burst into tears, which took us by surprise. "What's wrong, Sandy?" asked Vicki.

"This is so awful. I feel cooped up. If I could just go outside."

"We'd take you if it weren't so cold. What else can we do to cheer you up, Sandy?"

"I get scared when I think about the days to come. I'm not feeling very brave . . . I'm ashamed of myself."

"Oh, Sandy." And then we were all three crying.

"I don't want to go through this. It's too hard. What if I'm alone and choke? It's, it's scary."

"But the doctors promised they wouldn't let that happen to you."

"But I don't want that respirator or tubes. Why prolong this agony?"

"Sandy, those are decisions for a later time. Let's blow our noses and play cribbage, okay?" We waited several minutes for her to regain herself.

"Let's get out the good chocolate on the bottom shelf. I'm sorry for crying," she said in a child-like voice.

"It's okay, Sandy, we'll keep it among just the three of us."

Our visits often started this way, with a crying session. We understood this did not happen with others. Maybe she could let her fears turn into tears with us—new friends without a long history. Maybe the boundaries weren't so tight as with others. Maybe she felt safe in letting her emotions out with us. She'd always make us promise not to tell anyone.

On the drive home, we questioned why we felt better after our visits with Sandy, even though we were sadden by her situation.

"Maybe because we've come to know her so intimately."

"Yes, she trusts us in a different way, like showing her emotions when she won't with others."

"You know, I never felt like we were doing a sick woman a favor. It's like she did us a favor."

"How true. She's given us friendship . . . shared the richness of her experiences. . ."

"And opened up my eyes, at least, to what dignity of life means."

"Yep, you're right. She's also got me thinking about how to live life more graciously and without regrets."

"You know, I've been thinking—why don't we start a travel account and finally take a trip to a foreign country."

"I'm game. Let's do it and when we tell Sandy, we can ask for her advice—where, and when, and how."

"Oh, she'll love planning a trip for us."

Patsy

I became Sandy's gardener. Her room was like a florist shop, forever filled with flowering plants, expensive bouquets of roses, colorful cluster of summer garden flowers, but they didn't get tender, loving care. The staff typically over watered, I suppose thinking they then wouldn't have to do the chore as often.

In the earlier months, Sandy followed me in her wheelchair down to the kitchen at the end of the hall. I brought scissors, plant food and a small rake, and we would talk as I laid the flowers out on the table to cut stems anew, cull out the dead leaves, and fluff the dirt in the pots. We decided to save the plants by posting a sign—Do Not Water—on the windowsill.

As we'd go down the hall, Sandy tended to ignore the patients who were in varied stages of dementia. Little Estelle who would scream at people, Buck who tossed smutty remarks out to the females, Rose who made any person in sight a target for her wheelchair. One exception was Midge, the lady across the hall, who often joined us during the garden chores and would return with us to Sandy's room for treats. She was a pleasant, well-dressed woman and loved chocolate as much as Sandy. I noticed that Sandy offered See's chocolate to Midge rather than chocolate kisses. Boxes of this special candy arrived regularly from Mary in California, and Sandy kept them in the second drawer of the cabinet by her bed, the bagged candy visible on the bottom shelf.

As we were letting the second piece of chocolate melt in our mouths, a staff member walked into the room, clipboard in hand.

Sandy extended the box, "Just in time to share a sweet."

"Thanks, this is wonderful candy. Did you know that

you are getting a reputation as the chocolate lady? In fact, they call this room the chocolate shop."

"Well, I can see why," I said." I've come to think that Sandy's ministry in life goes hand-in-hand with chocolate."

"Well, food happens to be my reason for visiting you today," continued the staff person. "We need to remind everyone that our policy requires all foods to be in closed containers, with tight lids."

"What do you mean by all foods?" quizzed Sandy.

"It does include your candy. We are seeing evidence of small but unwanted residents, the unpopular mice."

"Oh, not to fuss about this room. Haven't you heard that the caffeine in chocolate kills mice? It might be your best weapon," informed Sandy.

The staff person looked dubious and her laugh came out as a giggle, "While that might be possible, we still have a policy we like to have followed. You can have the chocolate but please keep it in tight containers."

As she left the room, I asked Sandy, "Is that true about caffeine and mice?"

"Oh, I remember hearing that once. Thought it was a good reply, didn't you?"

We chuckled and I took on the task of finding the tight-lid containers for the chocolate.

E-Mail from Stan

To Mary and Jan: Yesterday was another one of those "reality check" days for Sandy. She didn't share what led up to her decision to take a stronger pain medication other than making a casual reference. We all know Sandy's aversion to any type of pill, so I assume the staff nurse may have been straightforward and ordered her to do so. After all, there is a limit to the amount of time the aides can massage her legs, which helps for the moment but not long term.

Her morning oxygen content was extremely low yesterday, which followed a night of difficult breathing. I hope she asks for the breathing mask at her next clinic visit. Her legs are twisting outward and her ankles bending inward. And, other muscles are beginning to weaken; noticeably her head is beginning to droop forward and to the left.

Carol

Upon Sandy's request, I visited her every week instead of every other week, my usual practice with other members of the congregation. My first thoughts presumed that she would want spiritual counseling, maybe a seeking of peace, or reflective conversation about her life. However, Sandy was not like others I had visited in similar situation. The only serious conversation touching on death was a discussion one afternoon on a book I had brought her to read; one I'd used for grief counseling during my pastoral years. *Loss of Dreams, A Special Kind of Grief* typically brought forth, from the reader, a re-shaping of life, perspective, and hope. The only personal comment she shared was: "I never saw heaven as a reward." Otherwise it was an academic discussion about the book rather than a personal discussion of facing her death. It puzzled me, for I knew her to be serious about her faith.

But then, how could hope be there, given the expressed nature of ALS. I guess I could understand the wish to enjoy this short period of time in close approximation to how she had always enjoyed life—socially with friends. I refrained from comments as I watched her live her days to the end dictated by a social calendar. The hours given to planning on how not to be alone kept a tight circle. The devotion of her family of friends was impressive and essential to her well-being.

People usually make peace with circumstances, letting go and accepting the end. I never saw Sandy get to that point. She was scared and kept the end at bay in a fashion that was uniquely hers. Even as the weeks became harder, she wanted to be brave or I wonder if it was a form of denial. It takes courage to share your inner thoughts, but it also takes courage to remain silent. I see that to die in dignity is to die in one's true character. And, I saw that Sandy remained true Sandy, proud, private, profound.

Sandy

My friend Ann, from Iowa, came for the last week of May to accompany me on my second clinic visit. She attentively wrote the notes for my medical journal that I kept at my desk and asked for clarification from the doctors on points I might overlook.

The first thing she noticed after greeting me was the medical identification bracelet I had to wear.

"Well, at long last I get to know what your given name is," she said.

"Why not still keep it my secret?" I asked as I held my hand over the plastic band.

"Not only have you not told me your name but you withheld your age also. It's been a joke with us since we met. You're so funny, Sandy."

"And if Stan hadn't hosted that 70th birthday party, you still wouldn't know my age."

"Well, I wasn't too surprised to find out we were close in age. I figured from your stories of earlier years that we must have been born not too many years apart. Now come on, let me see your name."

I held out my wrist and Ann said, "Oh, I can see why you like the name Sandy better, just as I like Ann better than my given name Gertrude."

"My mother really liked the name Virtue and if I'd been born second daughter instead of my sister, I would have had the name Joyce. Victoria, my second name, is a family name. We've had a Victoria every generation."

"You could have used it for a first name or why didn't you go by Vicki?"

"Oh, I got tagged with Sandy in high school and it sure was better than the grade school teachers calling me Virtue."

"Interesting in another way though, Sandy. The name Virtue surely matches your traits of kindness, generosity, integrity."

"Hold on, don't get carried away."

We were late for the early morning appointment, because the mobile van missed my pick-up time by forty-five minutes and then did another pick-up and delivery in St. Paul before heading towards the clinic. The medical team was the same as on the first visit, and they gave me their full attention and thoroughness in their questions and counsel. Even though we had thrown their schedule off, they did not rush their consultation. Ann was impressed with their thoughtfulness and conscientious manner.

My left arm was losing the ability to rise higher than my shoulder for which they prescribed new range-of-motion movements, along with detailed instructions for the therapist at Jones-Harrison. The dreaded test for lung capacity (a clip on my nose shut off nasal breathing as I exhaled every bit of breath from the lungs through my mouth— it was a painful procedure and one I detested) indicated quite a drop in capacity, although, the pulmonary doctor said my lungs were still operating in a 50-60% range. X-rays would determine if arthritis was the cause of the constant pain in my left hip, and thankfully, the x-rays could be done at the home. In any case, they wanted me to take pain medication regularly to minimize my pain. I have always shied away from medication, and it seemed I was now flooding my body with pills. I asked if the daily calcium tablets could be dropped, cause they were large and hard to swallow. Their okay made the number of pills a day decrease by two at least.

The doctors re-affirmed that added mechanical aids would be prescribed whenever I was ready. They described how the symptoms of oxygen privation would be noticed first at night; like I might wake up sharply out of sleep with shortness of breath or I would be unable to cough up the phlegm collecting in my throat. At that time, I would be fitted with a sleep mask meant to ease my breathing, and a device would be used to suction the mucus from my throat. When swallowing food and medication became too difficult, two things were suggested. One, puree the food and drink in liquid form. The other choice was inserting a feeding tube directly into the stomach for all nourishment and medication. If I thought either was needed prior to my next visit, all I had to do was call them directly or through the Jones-Harrison staff.

I reminded them again that I did not want extraordinary means used to prolong what was inevitable. The doctor assured me he knew of my wishes but would always introduce, describe, and propose procedures that would give me comfort and lessen physical distress. The choice was always mine as to what and when.

The information from the doctors gave Ann and I topics for discussion. Ann is a pretty straight arrow, direct person, unafraid to lay tough topics on the table for exploration, and she helped me re-think the doctors' suggestions without forcing me into a decision. Although, I knew I was far from ready to accept an apparatus for breathing or nourishment. Ugh!

We had our fun hours during the week. She helped me gussy up for a General Mills 25-Year Dinner on Wednesday evening and listened to my tales the next day. She went shopping for a cream to remove the dark shadow of hair on my upper lip, an outgrowth due to medication. What a laugh, sporting the milk mustache. "Maybe I could be fodder for a milk commercial." She shopped for stockings and soft slippers that would fit my swollen feet. She said she felt like the Prince kneeling before Cinderella as she tried them on. What didn't fit or suit my liking got returned. We shared our stories and remembered past events with laughter. I tried my sales skills to convince Ann to buy the lot in Bisbee, Arizona since she once had lived in Tucson. She had no interest, but I kept it a standard daily offer. "I'll give you a great deal." We bantered about the foolishness of this purchase my ex and I had made thirty years ago. We sat in the sunshine, and she would massage my legs for as long as I wished, which was until the pain diminished. We hadn't seen each other for three years but that didn't pose any kind of a void we had to fill. God it was good being with her again.

Patsy

I arrived at Jones-Harrison late Wednesday afternoon for a couple of hours with Sandy before Ann and I went off to dinner. I saw them sitting in the sun in the front garden as I walked towards the building. Ann was massaging the right leg, and I picked up the left one. Sandy was in top form, at ease and talkative.

I started laughing, "You'll love the news item I heard yesterday on morning public radio. A man and two women left a nursing home to drive to a nearby shopping mart. Thirteen hours later they were found lost and wandering in an adjacent state. The newscaster said: 'Yes, the man was driving.'"

"How the hell did they go thirteen hours?" asked Ann.

"Well, we know," Sandy reminded us, "no man would ever ask for directions."

"Patsy, are you sure you heard that story on the news?"

"Yep, I did."

"Men drivers!" Sandy quipped. "Same no matter what age."

"Patsy, you've never ridden in a car with Sandy, so you've missed out on her opinion of male drivers on the road," offered Ann.

"Sandy, I've heard this alluded about you before. Are men really low on your list?" I asked.

"Let me give you an example," Ann quickly took over the conversation. "First time this came up was on a September trip we took in Canada. But, I noticed the same opinion was voiced whenever Sandy was driving. It goes like this."

"Look at that idiot cut in front of me. Damn, men drivers."

"Sandy, I think it's a woman."

"Oh, men do it all the time, lousy drivers."

"Or I might hear, 'Look at that car racing off the entry ramp. Damn, men drivers!'"

"Sandy, it's a gal behind the wheel."

"Men do it all the time."

"Sandy, you make me laugh . . . blame for every mishap on the road is laid on men when most of the time we pass the car and it's a woman driver."

"Well, guess who they learned it from? Men!"

Ann

I left Minneapolis by way of Jones-Harrison. I wanted one more chance to be of assistance if needed and one more time to let her know I cared. It was a fortuitous decision. There were no errands to be done, just a few personal chores: put the silver earrings in the pierced ear lobes and clasp a silver and jet pendant over her black blouse, slip her black slippers on her feet, arrange her hair, review the notes from the clinic visit with the staff, and accept her thanks again for the shopping I'd done.

"Ann, here is a set of books that I thought you'd enjoy having."

I looked at the title *A Trilogy.* The set had three narrow books: *The Singer, The Song,* and *The Finale.* "I've never seen these or heard of this author, Calvin Miller."

"It's some of my favorite reading. Since you love books as much as I do, and you are beginning your literary writing, I wanted you to have these. They are a beautiful read. I re-read them last week so I'd be ready to give them to you."

"How many times have you read them?"

"Oh, maybe five or six times. The stories are a mythical retelling of the New Testament and were a nice compliment to my Bible studies. Wait, let me write a message for you on the inside cover."

"What a neat remembrance," as I read her words: *To Ann, my instant and everlasting friend. —Sandy.* "I imagine I shall be reading them as often as you did. It can be one mode of continued communication with you."

Just as the time approached for me to leave, she hinted that maybe I could tell her story, "Please make the title about how I died with dignity," she said. And I replied, "And, how about with courage, guts, and bravery." She made a reply, which I didn't hear through the sting of tears and emotions of good-bye. I backed out of the door looking eye to eye with Sandy. It seemed as if all of our times together were there in that very moment. She had been and still was a special person in my life.

Mary Ann

"Hi, here I am with our favorite butter burgers from Culver's and onion rings."

"What, no ice cream?"

"Now would I do that to you? Tonight it's a hot fudge malt."

"Great, I can handle that even though I had chocolate ice cream this afternoon. Jim and Madge were here."

"I've put the food down in the private eating area. If you're ready, let's go while things are still hot and cold." At the end of the hall was a full white kitchen, clean and inviting, open for common use. It had a glass table by the window looking out into a stand of trees, very cordial and attractive.

"How was your visit with your friend, Ann?" I asked as I unwrapped our burgers.

"It was good to see her. She hasn't changed, still has so much energy. Now, she wants to be a writer. Knowing her, she'll give it her all."

"Hey, look, new slippers."

"A bit of Ann's shopping. How was your week?"

"Hectic. The end of a school year always is busy with stuff. I'll miss your help this time. The teaching closets need sorting out. They are jammed."

"How so? We just re-organized them last year. Is it always a mess at the end of every year?"

"Yeah, I let the children get stuff out and when they help to put it back, well, you know how children do it. Just stuff it."

"When are you going up to the lake house? We usually went around this time, didn't we?"

"Funny you should ask. I'm leaving with Hooper early in the morning. I'm a little late opening it for this year. A bit reluctant, I guess, since I won't have you going with me."

"Yeah, because I do windows."

"Only the inside, you left me outside with the mosquitoes. At least, I won't have to wax the floors though, since you insisted upon doing them last year."

"Sorry I won't be your helper this year."

"It won't be all that hard. My brother was up there last weekend and did the heavy manual stuff."

"Would you put the cabin in the church auction again? Did it amount to much?"

"Not really, only $400. I'd hoped that we'd raise more than that for the BeFrienders group."

"Who ended up with the highest bid?"

"Glad we limited it to four . . . Carol, Evelyn, Sara, and Laurie."

"Well, I sort of left you in the lurch, since we were to be the chief cooks and bottle washers for them."

"It'll work. I'm sure they won't be able to stay out of the kitchen."

"What a lot of great memories from all the times we

spent there. You always chided me about the stack of books I brought along, but that porch was a great reading spot, day and night. I'll be thinking of our past visits and wish I was there with you, even washing windows and floors."

"And Hooper is going to miss lap time with you on the drive up."

"He's so funny . . . how he sits looking out the window like a real sightseer."

"These burgers are good, glad I didn't have time to cook a casserole this week."

"Speaking of food, I've written out the menu for the church cooks. Would you mind taking charge?"

"Can do. How many of your favorite foods are being served? Bet chocolate and ice cream for sure."

"Well of course and along with the rest of my favorites. Deviled eggs, and I wrote out my recipe for them."

"They'll get a kick out of that. What else?"

"A large platter of olives of every kind, black, Spanish, green. Brunswager sandwiches . . . "

I cut her off, "Are you sure that everyone is as big a fan of Brunswager as you?"

"Probably not, so there'll be a plate of cold cuts and cheeses and a couple of salads, a pasta and tossed green. I thought it would nice to have some of my sea shells on the table for decorations."

"Where are the other shells? Remember mine were some of the best and beautiful of the collection. I still plan to use them for a still-life painting."

"Stan has the rest of them. There were a lot of shells, so if anyone wanted to take one as a memento, I'd like that. Most of them were found on Sanibel Island. I probably told you about Pat, my old next-door neighbor who had a condo there. I became her annual winter visitor. After she died, our Patty joined me a couple of times in Florida and also California. We walked the shore, early morning, in search for shells."

"Interesting how travel and trips intertwine with many of your friendships. Also, it's interesting how many of your friends are named Jim and Pat."

"Yes, guess that's true." Sandy pushed away her plate. "I can't eat the rest of the burger, why not take it home for Hooper."

"By the way, we should set a time to work on the bio. When I get back, eh?"

"Okay, I've jotted down a little already."

Sandy

Mary Ann was my first, youngest and closest friend at church. The three decades between our ages was of no consequence. Our friendship was seeded in church projects we co-chaired and bloomed over the summer vacations at her family cottage in northern Minnesota. Mary Ann is a peaceful, quiet personality with no evidence ever of hard edges. She has creative talent that comes forth in her interior decorations, entertainment, and artist easel. While I read my books, she painted still life or beautiful landscapes. I was pleased when my old friends welcomed her into our family group.

E-mails

Dear Sandy,

Any chance of you wanting company Saturday, June 21st in the evening and also Sunday, the 22nd? Bart and I will be visiting old friends in Michigan and I could fly over to see you. Stan has offered to pick me up and put me up. We're off to Nevada for three days

of R & R and gambling. I'll call you next week to see if you like my little surprise.
Love, Jan

Hi Jan,
So excited for June 21st to come. Can't wait!!! Give Bart a hug for me . . . and I'll give you yours when you get here. Hurry!!!!!
Love, Sandy

Stan

My mind was in a whirl with ideas to make the June weekend a smashing hit. I could sense the pleasure Sandy would have if we could visit some of her favorite haunts when Jan was here. She wanted to add Glyn, Jim, and Patty and we'd make a party of six. Now, how to get a van having the equipment for Sandy's needs and width of her wheelchair. No luck with a Minneapolis rental. Everything that qualified was already booked, and I hesitated to tell her that we'd have to do the weekend in Jones-Harrison.

However, the gods do look favorably upon us some times. Later in the day, I received a callback from one of the rental companies. They had located a van for that weekend, but it would have to be picked up in St. Cloud. "What the hell, it's only an hour drive up and another one back." I told them, "Yes, we'll take it." Glyn and I would pick it up on Friday afternoon and return it late Sunday.

Louiva

Sandy often remarked how lonely it was in the evening. She had friends who came for dinner and stayed through the early evening, but those later hours hung heavy. Once Sandy knew that my husband and I were night owls just like she, her invitation came with the hint about the main front doors being open until nine o'clock. The night visits suited our schedule perfectly. We'd slip in before nine, stay past eleven and be home by midnight.

Sandy found it interesting that my husband was the third Jim she knew. "We call one Big Jim to distinguish him from Jim, the husband of Marge. Now what can we tag you with?"

"How about James," Jim suggested. "Sounds a bit English, don't you think?"

"You were Jimmy when I first met you," I offered.

"Maybe I'll use the first letter of your last name and refer to you as Jim P.," Sandy decided.

"No, sounds like I'm doing it rather than being it. Better you just call me by my last name, Puffer."

We made a good evening threesome. Working her puzzles was a challenge. Jim and I never found more than two or three pieces in an hour. Sandy spotted pieces easily but asked us to place them, as her hands didn't hold the pieces tightly. We often played a few hands of rummy or shared the genealogy of our ancestors. Jim's great-grandfather was a doctor, born in New York but buried in Minnesota. His practice began in Taylor's Fall with Indians, and he told a fascinating story about the first patient who came to him with an ax in the middle of his torso. We never knew the end of the tale, whether he lived or died. Sandy also had a pioneer in her family, a great-grandfather who came from Wisconsin to North Dakota where he drove the first stagecoach routes. These histories led to interesting speculations.

We held hands as we said our "good-nights" following a practice we did in church when giving a blessing for the day. Sandy held on tight as she said, "Please Lord, watch over these two dear friends that their lives may be continuously blessed with health and happiness. May they have love in abundance as a measure of the love they have given me. I thank them for their hours of friendship."

We'd known her from the first day we attended church services, and Jim worked with her on several projects. We counted her among our dearest of friends.

Jeannie

"Bet you've wondered what has happened to me. This is Jeannie."

"Yes and no," said Sandy. "So good to hear your voice. Are you coming by?"

"No, these last months have been a challenge, and I apologize for being so invisible to you."

"I suppose I could have wondered if you ran off with my treasures. Such a laugh, eh?"

"Well that's why I'm calling. I wanted you to know that your last items for sale are now out on eBay."

"Any bids?"

"Unfortunately not. There is so much stuff for sale. I'm not sure how people can even zoom in on any particular item."

"I wonder if I could get on eBay on the computer here?"

"I would think so. You'd want *www.ebay.com.* Maybe someone could help you. It's not really difficult. You have to do a lot of scrolling under chocolate sets to find your twenty-eight piece set."

"You suppose we should adjust the price?"

"Well, let's wait awhile and see if we get any interest first. We can always price down. I'll be checking with you again later next week. I'm working myself out from under a mountain of paperwork so we can take off for four days of golf at Grandview Lodge."

"Trust you'll have a hole in one, as reward for all your help with the sale of my stuff. Call me whether you have good news or not. Better yet, stop by, would love to see you."

Jan

Stan had said he'd meet me. I didn't see him but I saw Big Jim looking between the heads of the crowd as I walked through Gate Four at the airport. I waved my hand.

"Hi big guy. So glad the plane finally got here."

"So am I, since we're curbed parked."

"I expected to see Stan. Is everything okay?"

"Yes. He's with the car. We did an early lunch elsewhere when we heard your plane would be late and then drove around the hills on the other side of the river. We got here about fifteen minutes ago," Jim responded as he took the small suitcase from my hand.

"What's teed up for the weekend?"

"Just you wait and see."

"How's Sandy doing?"

"Holding her own right now, although you will notice the droop of the head and weakness in the left hand. She's really looking forward to your visit and being out on parole, as she puts it."

Jim opened the terminal door and pointed directly straight ahead. I noticed that a van was at the curb with its side door open. As we approached, I could see Sandy looking out, stretched forward with a gleaming smile on her face. It was a most beautiful sight and unexpected.

"Wow, what a surprise to see you here."

"Hop in. There are more surprises to come. Too bad Bart had to stay on in Michigan, I'd always wanted to treat him to Minneapolis."

Hugs all around, before I climbed into the back seat. They'd spent a good part of the day on the Wisconsin side of the Mississippi where they'd had lunch earlier at a restaurant on the Croix River, one of Sandy's favorite spots. She repeatedly remarked that she had not expected to cross the Mississippi again. It wasn't hard to see that she was on a high just to be out and about. Since it was late afternoon, we drove out to the west side of the city for an evening on the verandah of Lord Fletchers overlooking Lake Minnetonka, everybody's favorite for dining out. Sandy was our host for the evening and had arranged for dinner to be served just at sunset. And of course, that included walleye, the Minnesota noted fish.

Patty's toast this evening: "A friend's eyes are a good mirror."

Sandy

For sure, the highlight of the summer was the weekend visit with Jan. The six of us made it a memorable time. They took me places I never thought I would enjoy again.

Lunch across the river at Prescott where the Saint Croix and Mississippi meet (everyone singing "Ole Man River" in full voice).

Sunset at Lord Fletcher's (even a few customers joined us in signing "By The Light Of The Silvery Moon" . . . keep a shining in June. . .).

Barbecue ribs at Famous Dave's (dear Stan arranging to have smaller water glasses that I could handle, rather than the usual large, heavy ones).

A drive through the University Arboretum where

flowerbeds were alive in their colors (Glyn popping out of the van to quickly snip a lavender iris for me).

A starlight drive in downtown Minneapolis and singing "When You're Smiling" on the way home. Sunday services at church, and back to the Mall of America for another dinner of ribs.

All possible because Stan was able to rent a mobile van to transport me in the wheelchair. Patty saw a snazzy black, flat top hat with a narrow brim at the mall. She bought it for Stan, the chauffeur. We tucked mementoes of the day in the red band. Being out in the activities of normal life gives one a sense of being normal. The three days were a temporary suspension, as if a judge had given me a brief reprieve from my sentence. When we took Jan to the airport, I knew we'd not have other days like these again.

Jan

I elected to stay the night with Sandy. Since we were both night owls, we stretched our bedtime out to several hours after midnight. It was like a slumber party. Insignificant girl talk, pedicures and painting toe nails in bright red polish, a late-night comic television show, and a re-visit to the good times in San Diego with Bart. The night nurse brought in chocolate chip cookies and coffee she'd made in the small kitchen off the foyer. We had enough caffeine to keep us on a high and wide-awake. When Sandy finally settled into bed, I stretched out on the recliner for the few hours until daybreak and our last day together. I realized I was saying goodbye to one of the most charming personalities I'd known. I slept lightly as if I wanted to stay conscious of her in these last moments we were together.

Patty

Sandy's strength and mobility for attending Sunday services at her church, if not over, were down to the last few. Yesterday several of us attended church with her, making their services our services for the day. Sandy had made arrangements and planned a luncheon for twelve in the church hall. Pastor Carol and several of the parishioners were invited to join us for a lunch menu of pasta and chicken salad. It was good to see Vicki and Amy again; the two young women who volunteered to stay nights with Sandy at her house last November and December. And I met the guy from church who moved Sandy's furniture from upstairs to downstairs and then to Jones-Harrison. I could see that this was Sandy's way to show appreciation to those of the congregation who had been there so willingly to help her. True Sandy, all the way, to dignify their deeds and say her thanks with food.

Sandy

Dearest Jan,

This picture should bring back memories of Lord Fletchers and good friends. Miss you like crazy. Feel like we are soul mates.

My breathing is getting tough—and I can't talk long on the phone anymore. Or write much either for that matter.

Hope things are going well for you guys.

Love to you both,
Sandy

P.S. Mary is coming the 19th of September.

P.P.S. Did you get the caramel recipe to Lynn? Maybe she'll supply you with Christmas candy.

Mary Ann

When I entered her room, she was dozing in the wheelchair, relaxed from a therapy session. She said the hot packs applied to her upper back always made her sleepy. I put the container holding our lunch on the windowsill and headed for the recliner to read. I moved quietly, but Sandy has a phenomenal sense of knowing when someone is in the room. Her lids opened and her eyes sought me out. She gave her signature smile, like a child who's just witnessed magic.

"Hi, so good to see you. You here for lunch?"

"Yes, indeed. I brought a chicken rice dish that we can warm up in the kitchen. How was your sleep last night?"

"Not too bad, awake just once. I had to go to the bathroom, and it took some time before the aids were here to help me. I almost peed in bed. I'm going to quit drinking anything after dinner."

"That's not a good idea, you know. Your body needs the liquid."

"But what a fuss getting rid of it." She shook her head in disgust.

"Are you in the mood to work on the bio? I have paper and pen ready."

"Yeah, but let's get out of this room. Why don't we go down to the lounge area by the kitchen."

The session was like pulling teeth; she was so stingy with personal history. I tried to get her to flesh out the achievements of her life, and she acted as though there'd been none. She is so modest and ignored any encouragement I gave for her to toot her horn. She was adamant that there be no mention of her ex nor any part of their twenty-some years together. She downplayed her achievements with General Mills, so what was dictated to me read like an obituary: just the facts about birth, raised on a farm, education, years at work, political affiliations, and church.

"This certainly does not portray the real you, the fun-loving traveler, your aspirations and accomplishments, the things you are proud of, a personal message," I complained.

"If others see those things as true and want to tell them, then let them do so."

I shook my head and said, "Then I'll have to get creative with these words of remembrance if I am going to be the reader. Why, oh why, is it so difficult for you to be complimentary of yourself?"

"Guess that's another tale not to be told. Let's dish up your chicken creation." And that was the end of that subject.

Sandy

I awaited Stan's daily call to ask, "Stan, can you come for dinner tomorrow and then spend the evening with me?"

"What's up?" I could imagine the quizzical look he'd have on his face.

"I'm ready to review everything I've arranged for the service. I really look to you and Mary Ann to carry through, you realize."

"Sandy, do you really feel up to this right now? Mary Ann did brief me on what you've planned." No answer. "We could do it later. You're not checking out this week, are you?"

"No, but I just want to put this stuff to bed, so I don't have to think about it any more."

"Ah, put it into our hands and let us think about it, right?"

"Of course, I trust you implicitly."

"Guess I'll let your compliment pull rank this time. I do have my remembrance written. Would you like me to read it to you tomorrow?"

"Ycs, and I think I'd like Mary Ann to hear it also."

"Well, why not ask her to join us, if not for dinner, then afterwards?"

"Okay, I bet she will."

It was the end of June, I had talked with all those who I wished to take part in the memorial, chosen a lunch menu of my favorite foods, compiled information for the obituary notice, written my floral order for lavender flowers . . . lilacs if they could be gotten, and violets (my sister Joyce's favorite) . . . and set the agenda for the services with Carol. The only task remaining was sorting through hundreds of photographs and putting them into a display depicting my times with friends. My plan was to host a weekend photo party, inviting Marilyn, Stan, Mary Ann, Patty, Marge and Jim.

I'll tie that down tomorrow night. *How odd it feels to be saying good-bye to oneself.*

Stan

"I've always thought a eulogy could be reverent or irreverent, serious or humorous, religious or worldly, but above all it must be honest. I wrote with a bit of each of those things in my words, overlaid with a meed of praise."

"Mead? How does that fit in there?" asked Sandy

"Have you never seen it in one of your crossword puzzles?"

"Yes, but the clue is usually, fermented honey drink. How does that fit in? Are you giving a drunken praise?"

"We must be talking two different words. Mine is spelt meed."

"Meed? What clue would have been given?"

"One might have been 'a fitting return' or maybe recompense . . . an earned reward."

"Okay, so you one-upped me this time."

"Seems I add a new word to my vocabulary every time I listen to you, Stan," chuckled Mary Ann. "The last one was modicum, which by the way fits more often than not. I used it in class, and now twenty students have added it to their vocabulary."

"That's a bit optimistic for young students," I replied. "Lucky if it was only one or two, Mary Ann."

"Well, one boy did say 'seems that modicum was the same as smidgen.' He said he preferred smidgen."

"Okay," said Sandy, "I think I'm ready, but let's close the door."

I put the box of Kleenex and bowl of chocolate on the stand by Sandy's chair. "Let's not sit too close together . . . give ourselves some space," I said as I took the seat by the windows. Mary Ann moved to the recliner chair out of direct line of sight to Sandy.

I held back a few seconds, coughed, took a sip of water and began, "I'll first open one of two hat boxes that I will have by my side. I put on your black hat with the rose and short veil that you last wore at your 70th birthday party, and I tuck a black kerchief in my breast pocket. And, thus I begin.

"I am Stan Kolden, and if there is one thing I learned from Sandy in the twenty-six years we were neighbors, is that a good hat makes any event even better. This was one of her vintage best!

"So much to hear, so much to know, so many interesting facts and stories, so little time. So true of all of us. Life is just too busy and too often we just don't listen, we just don't learn, we don't make the really important things of life a priority. We just don't take the time.

"It was no different for Sandy. But for most of us we would never know that *because* she did take the time to make each of us a priority in some way, her own way.

"As a consumer relations leader at General Mills, do you really think that Betty Crocker-Weisenburger (yes, it is a hyphenated name, little known to anyone, most especially the boy executive group at the top) . . . do you really think that Sandy really cared if your cake mix didn't work exactly right? Probably not. But she most certainly did care that as a consumer, you would ultimately feel good about the customer service you received to your complaint. She lived and breathed that kind of caring for and about the people around her, whether you were a stranger or a close friend. A virtue I envy.

"So where did that wonderful virtue of picking the right things in life to care about come from? The answer is very simple . . . North Dakota!

"I warn you now that there will be a test, so you had better be taking notes. And, there will be no snickering, because I too am from North Dakota, so I know of what I speak.

"So what about North Dakota . . . other than being Santa's first stop on his way from the North Pole . . . God's country, wonderful people, community spirit, real family values, faith, hope and charity; virtues played out everyday by ordinary people, no class distinctions.

"But even more important that that, a defining moment, 'way back then, in a land far away' two loving parents brought baby Sanderson to a baptismal font, not unlike this one before us, and were asked, "What do you name this child?" Virtue Victoria Sanderson was their

reply. So this child of God . . . empowered with the Holy Spirit . . . lived out her calling, her ministry, the good virtues of life. And, we all have been touched.

"Being a product of North Dakota is certainly an advantage but also no guarantee to a blessed life of smooth sailing and happy days. For it was from the prairie that a young man named Weisenburger turned her head, caught her fancy and made her Missus.

"Years later, it was that same man who betrayed the very virtues and trust on which her life was based. A hurtful experience, long in healing . . . it was about this time that I met Sandy.

"It was in the late '70s when I bought the townhouse across the courtyard from her townhouse. I came to know that the woman across the patio proudly wore an 'I hate men' attitude. There was no welcome wagon coming from her door to mine. More likely a patio door closing if I would come out upon the scene. Her cats, the love and joy of her life, would be scurried inside so as not to meet this strange man who had invaded her territory.

"Now strange does certainly describe me, but at least once in awhile, wonderful can be attached. The process was slow and guarded, but two years later the seeds of friendship began to grow. Years later, I heard the history of her marriage, and the story of the baby who died. It was then I began to realize how those hurts influenced her life. Her home church had left her, and in classic Sandy style she so clearly communicated 'up your nose with a rubber hose.' She moved on in life, quite successfully, without men and without a church.

"Our friendship, both strange and wonderful, grew to a time where I knew I'd been honored with the title of friend. I was invited to buy a time slot, along with other friends, with Mavis for a body massage in Sandy's lounge room downstairs. Mavis was the person who invited Sandy to this church where the gift of the Holy Spirit, planted so long ago at the church on the prairie, blossomed again. It was my pleasure to be one of a few to be here the Sunday Sandy joined this fellowship of believers. And, as it's said, the rest is history.

"Hurt, pain, disappointment . . . realities of life. When my office phone would ring mid-afternoon and Sandy said she needed to go to a movie and sit in the dark, I knew she had had a bad day. Did we talk about it? Of course not! We're from North Dakota where you don't actually talk about troubles of life. You just suck up and live through it. Betty Crocker-Weisenburger would smile, but just like the rest of us, she had her moments. It was in those moments of humanness, vulnerability and blunt honesty that our friendship grew and flourished.

"There were plain and simple unquestioned givens. All men, with a few exceptions, continued to be stupid, and all Democrats were most certainly of the devil. But you know, even with the blessed virtue of North Dakota, we are not perfect. That's part of the package deal, born into sin. But, she made the very best effort at making a positive difference in so many lives. Most especially, through this church, her work at General Mills, in politics, volunteerism and the quality time she gave her friendships."

I paused to tell Sandy and Mary Ann, "I'll now take off the black hat, open the other box, put on your favorite red hat with the large satin bow and exchange the black handkerchief for a red one. Time to lighten up, similar to what the red hat clubs do." I didn't give time for a response.

"It was her tradition after Christmas Eve church services to come home and begin to write her Christmas greetings to friends far and wide . . . she'd be up most of the night, not ending until all cards and envelopes were ready for mailing. Yes, she was a night owl, and often as I was on a 3:00 A.M. trip to the bathroom, I would look out my bedroom window and see her lights, as she worked on yet another project for some person or group.

"The bad news of the ALS diagnosis was communicated in her last Christmas letter, far different than previous Christmas letters telling of good times traveling. From that short but to the point letter, her investment of love returned to her everyday. The mail, doorbell, and phone brought to Sandy caring letters and cards, visits, good old North Dakota hot dishes, countless caregivers with hugs of compassion, love, and support.

"For us, twenty-six years of potluck suppers, watching Hallmark commercials side by side while saying, 'don't look, don't look' as tears ran down our faces . . . deaths of family members and loved ones . . . sharing our friends and church communities, even some friends and an occasional Democrat, were all glued together with ice cream and chocolate.

"Sandy finally let me into the lives of her cats. We shared their furry and unconditional loving purrs and said good-bye to dear pets together. We often commented, "What did Jesus do with all the dead cats?"

"Virtue Victoria Sanderson-Weisenburger, certainly a wonderful story. A woman of integrity, love, compassion and virtue . . . a ministry for and to all she touched with her life. Well-done, good and faithful servant. So much to hear, so much to know . . . so little time . . . so true for all of us . . . learning to take the time . . . a virtue exemplified."

I didn't tell her that I planned to place the red hat on the urn of ashes. We sat silently for several minutes, time to use several Kleenex's. Finally, Sandy spoke in a weak voice, "I believe you talk too much, Stan."

"I'm not changing a word."

"Wonder if I insist."

"Then, I'll not read a memorial to Sandy."

"Okay, but I'll be there to make sure you read it as is."

"Afraid I might include a secret or two?"

"I know you, Stan. Can't resist a surprise." Sandy motioned towards the bowl. "How about some chocolate while maybe we change a few words."

"I like it," Mary Ann whispered.

With that reading that day, I'd said my good-bye to Sandy. I was proud of the words and pleased that I could get them read without a major breakdown. It was a real test. If I could read them here, I felt I could read them at the memorial.

Sandy

I am a chocolate-holic, as was my brother Lawrence. Chocolate, in any form, is an all time favorite treat. My friends cater to my addiction, bringing me brownies, chocolate chip cookies, chocolate malts and keeping my candy bowl full of chocolate kisses. We all—visitors, aides, nurses, me—have our hands in the bowl. The day would arrive I'd be counted out, when my throat muscles couldn't swallow the denseness of chocolate, and my addiction could no longer be fed.

My voice was losing strength, getting weaker in tone and length of speaking time. Eating had become more difficult and food was taken in tiny amounts. I became selective in what and how much I ate. The food on my dining trays was barely touched unless a person was in the room to force-feed me. My coughing reflexes were weak in bringing up phlegm, holding me in a constant worry about choking on food.

My hands were losing their strength, particularly the left one. No grip. Cups and glasses slipped and broke. The range of motion of the left arm was all but gone, and I couldn't comb my hair. My head drooped forward towards the left shoulder causing a constant back pain from muscles trying to keep my head up straight. In fact, I noticed that my whole body was beginning to slump to the left.

I tire easily and physical energy is in short supply. I stay in bed later in the morning, waiting longer to get dressed. Putting on clothes has become a chore, but my vanity will not allow me yet to spend the day in a hospital gown.

I wish it were over. I feel dull and so useless . . . living in a half-dead body that is worthless. Imagine all the dollars being paid for nurses and aids to take care of such a lifeless object. Guess I'm ready to let go of the physical . . . not so my spirit and soul. I wonder how aware I will be of my spirit when the last breath is taken. Just look at your self, Sandy, death is hardly scary anymore. God, it will be a blessing. Be merciful. Please keep my hand in Yours.

Karen and Myra

We drove into Minneapolis on Friday for the July holiday weekend, arriving in time for dinner with Larry and Sandy and, at her request, stayed through Monday. Most people in Minneapolis go out of town for this holiday, so we had Sandy pretty much to ourselves.

On Saturday, Sandy had errands for us to do and suggested a pizza party in her room with afternoon visitors, if there'd be any. She'd reserved the mobile van for Sunday morning, cause she wanted us all to go to church services with her. Later, we found that she had a specific reason for us staying a day longer; she was disposing of her last cherished items.

"Girls, I want my personal things to find a home with those who will treasure them. Please choose what you'd like of the items in this room and those that are in a safe deposit box."

"Oh, Sandy, do we have to do this now?"

"Yes, we do. My time is getting shorter, not longer, and I want the enjoyment of seeing what you select."

"Gosh, you make it so final."

"Well girls, I guess it is. But, it's important to me that you have first choice." We glanced around the room while Sandy told us, "The only piece in the room spoken for is the large painting of seashells. It belongs to Patty with whom I shared so many sea-side walks at Sanibel Island."

"I'd love to have the family photo of our grandparents," said Myra, as she picked up the framed picture from the shelf. "Mother had a few but not the portrait of them in their wedding attire. Would that be okay with you two?" Myra asked.

"Yes," replied Karen and Larry nodded. "Father's album had quite a few of grandpa and grandma."

"Well, you have the next couple of days to make your selections, and I'll tell you the story that goes with them. Although, I bet you've heard most of them before," added Sandy.

"You don't want us to take them now, do you?" asked Karen.

"Yes, you could, or we can put your name on the pieces. There are other things I'd like you girls to have." She paused a moment. "I've kept most of my good jewelry in a safe deposit box. I'd rather you choose what you like, and of course, I'd like to hear why they appealed to you."

"Is this why you wanted us to stay over?" asked Myra.

"Yes, somewhat. Larry has the power of attorney to authorize entry to the box, and he said Monday would be a good day for him."

"If we could make it mid-morning. I have a meeting I should be at by one thirty," Larry said.

"Okay, we'll meet you there. Sandy can give us directions."

"That will work fine," replied Larry. "I'm closing the box and you can bring what's left here."

"Not a good idea to keep valuables in your room, Aunt Sandy," Karen warned.

"Of course not. We ain't that dumb," Larry tossed back. "They have boxes here, downstairs."

"Now, now children, no squabbling."

Karen and Myra

"Aren't they beautiful?" said Myra as she held up emeralds.

"Didn't she buy those on the South American trip?"

"Which one, I wonder. Brazil or Peru?"

"Well, I remember that the amethysts came back from the trip she took with Mary down the Amazon. Look there are earrings, a necklace and an unset stone. What a deep, deep purple they are," said Karen as she cradled the jewels in her hand.

"Not a mark in the stone. It's absolutely gorgeous."

"I know you love amethyst, Myra. Will this be your pick?"

"No, I don't think so. I have several pieces already in

my jewelry box. Gosh, so many beautiful gems, and we've never seen them on Sandy."

"Look, here's a box marked 'cameos,'" Myra said as she slipped the rubber band off and opened the lid. "Oh, remember when she showed these to us at one of our all-girl weekends."

"Yes. I was with her when she purchased this large black one at an antique store along Lake Pepin. Did she ever give you a cameo?"

"Yes, a lovely small coral cameo that I wear on a gold chain."

"She gave me the white cameo that Aunt Joyce gave her as a birthday present when they were younger."

"That was mother's. I wouldn't mind having it some day as a memento. When did she give it to you?" asked Myra.

"I think the year when only I got a Christmas present."

"Yeah, how well I remember that holiday. You were the only niece or nephew who received a gift, because you were the only one who'd sent her a thank you note for the previous Christmas gifts."

"We have to admit, she does live by her principles, eh?"

"Karen, what do you think about this sapphire? I'd have a ring setting designed for it."

"It's a different kind of blue, isn't it? It's so dark and the center star is light blue."

"This is my choice, and since we can have two, I'll choose this small diamond ring. It looks dramatic set in the white gold. What do you think of it on my pinky?"

"Nice. Dainty piece. I'm going to stay with the three pieces of amethyst."

Sandy

"Well, you surprise me a bit," I said looking at the jewelry they'd laid on the bed. "I thought one of you might have chosen the pearls from Asia. But, I assume you are pleased with your choices."

"Yes," replied Karen, "especially since I thought Myra would want the amethysts."

"Mary and I found them separately while on our trip down the Amazon. The loose stone in a village along the water way and the necklace and earrings in a jewelry store on the boat. The man in the village stall wanted us to buy more. I think he saw a couple of easy tourists."

"Sandy, where did this small diamond ring come from?" asked Myra. "I've never seen you wear it."

"No, suppose not. It was one of the last few gifts your uncle gave me before the divorce, and I swore none of his jewelry would drape my body again. Don't know why I didn't dispose of it before now, but I'm glad that it will be with you."

"Is it for the same reason that the sterling silver set is in the vault? Because it was a part of your marriage? Larry said he's never seen you use it for any of the dinners you hosted at your house."

"I suppose not. Trouble with keeping things in a bank is that you rarely use the things that you keep there. I should have kept the silver at the house and used it. I'd like Larry to have the set but he hasn't taken it yet. Anything else I have here that you'd like?" asked Sandy.

"Maybe," said Myra. "I've always admired those two small pictures from Vienna. And, you also said that there was a brooch that was Grandma Jenny's."

"They're yours. My jewelry box is in that second drawer. You'll find the brooch in there. Mother always wore it on a gray dress. The jet-black stone really showed nicely against the gray. I think it was her favorite piece. Anything else you'd like, Karen?"

"No, I'm happy with what I have."

"I think each of you ought to have pearls also. How about the small bracelet? There's one for each of you."

"Oh Sandy, this is so strange, so sad," words said with choking hesitation. "Thank you so much for what you've given us all your life."

"Oh, please, girls don't do this. I have to hold on. Let's head off downstairs, I made reservations in the dining room for lunch."

"We do have to be on our way right afterwards."

"I know. It's a long drive. Just promise that you will come back again, soon. Please?"

Sandy

Photographs were strewn across the room for most of the week. All those who came to visit spent time viewing old pictures of my life. We moved the vases and flowers to the back of the windowsill to make room for the sorting. Mary Ann and Stan were with me when we started on Friday morning; they made labels of five different categories.

"How many picture boards do you think there ought to be?"

"Well, the question is how many segments of your life do we want to segregate."

"Family and friends could be the distinction."

"But that wouldn't depict the full scope of your life."

"Why don't we work them around the activities you loved the most?"

"Good idea, Mary Ann," said Stan. "How about this?

One each for community, politicians, no, no, no it's country plus family and friends."

"Well, don't forget my church."

"Great. Let's tape those labels to the windowsill, and we'll assemble pictures by category. It will be easier to sort out the photos you want to display," suggested Stan. "With as many albums and boxes you have, you may be busy for a while."

"I figure that it will be a good task to do with my visitors. Some of the pictures probably will evoke stories and laughter."

Mary Ann held up the folders containing all the pictures of people who had visited or assisted me since last December. "What about these? Shouldn't they be in a separate category?"

Stan jumped up waving his hands, "I've got it. I've got it."

I raised my eyebrows, looked at him and said, "This will be showy, I bet."

"Let's have the last board titled 'Love Returned.' Wouldn't that complete the story?"

The two of them out-voted me, so that's the way we went. The hours that stretched into days going through photos were a review of many years. What an immense sense of gratitude I felt, my life had been abundant and rich in experiences and people. Odd, how feelings of gratitude and pain can reside in the same place at the same time.

Glyn

I came into Sandy's room to find her gazing at photos she held in her hands. "What a surprise to see you at midday," she said with a smile, looking up my tall lanky frame.

"You know what I like about you? You're never without that charming smile."

I winked at her. "Only have a couple of minutes, I'm on my way back to the office."

"Have a seat. Move that box."

"In the midst of pictures, aren't you?"

"I've been sortin' all morning. Down to just these last few which aren't for display."

"Who is this?" I asked as I reached for the photos. "We haven't seen him before in any other picture."

"Right, he hasn't been in my life since the sixties."

"Is this your ex?"

"Yes."

"Guess I'm surprised that you have any relic of him at all. I thought I understood that he had been expunged from your life."

"I'm not sure why I couldn't toss these few pictures," Sandy said slowly. "I burnt all the rest."

"Nice looking guy."

"Yeah, guess the other woman thought so too. Hand me the scissors, I need to make sure that they don't end up on any of the picture boards."

"I highly doubt, Sandy, that your friends would pull one like that on you."

I watched as she snipped the photos and relished the thought that she had kept something of him. Her animosity towards marriage was so great and seemed to me to be an indication of how much she'd loved and trusted him. I know she's teased a lot about her bitterness towards men, but there must have been a soft spot somewhere within her to have kept these pictures. I warmed to this touch of humanness in her and loved her all the more for it. Under that protective shield she wore on the outside, a tender heart remained inside.

Stan

"I heard that you popped in to see Sandy today," I said, as we met for dinner at the St. Louis Grill. "That's not a typical time for your visits."

"Well, I was on my way back to the office from a meeting on the west side of the city. I grabbed a quick and early lunch giving me extra time. Then since I was passing by Jones-Harrison, thought I'd just stick in my head for a hello."

"What was going on?"

"I couldn't stay long, but she was alone. Several friends were coming after lunch to look over the pictures sorted on the windowsill."

"Did she get to the bottom of the box?"

"Yes, the big surprise was at the bottom of the box."

"Like what?"

"Four pictures of her husband."

"You're kidding?"

"Nope."

"She's always claimed to have saved no reminders of him," I said with a shake of my head. "I'm surprised that she let you see them."

"Well, there were four. One when he was young, maybe graduation. Two of both of them, one was a studio picture. He was a good-looking guy."

"What did she say? Do?"

"She said she didn't know why she'd kept them. Said she had burnt all the rest. I wondered if she'd wanted to preserve a bit of her love for him. Of course, I didn't inquire."

"Sandy has never shared too many stories of her life with him or of her marriage, with me or anyone else. Patty,

I think might be the only one who knew him since they were still a married couple when she first met Sandy."

"She cut the photos into small pieces today."

"Why am I surprised?" I sipped my wine. "Sandy has always been such a private person, so secretive except for her opinions. I continually had to look for small clues, watch her behavior, and then piece together what might be going on within her."

"You've been a close neighbor friend for years, does she not share herself now, particularly with death at her bedside?"

"No, that would not be Sandy. I've wondered if this is a just another scenario she can't go near."

"How's that?"

"I think back to the time of her brother's heart attack. I found her behavior peculiar and a mystery. She'd adored Lawrence and they'd been very close throughout their lives. She visited him in Arizona several times a year and relied upon him for advice. I remember the afternoon she got word that he was in the hospital in Phoenix. She came over immediately, visibly shaken, sobbing, needing to be with someone."

Glyn waited for me to continue.

"I quickly swung into action getting flight times and offered to drive her to the airport. I told her that I and another one of our close neighbors would take care of the house. I just presumed she'd want to be on her way quickly, as the heart attack was a serious one."

"Did she get there in time?"

"The short of it was that she did . . . not . . . go to Arizona. I couldn't figure it out, for she loved him dearly. I could never ferret out the reason why. It just puzzled me."

"Maybe she thought he had more time."

"Oh, I think not. They didn't expect him to last the week."

"Are death and dying things she can't deal with? Some people can't, you know."

"I suspect that might be true. She ignores talking about death, no discussion, never ever says the word."

"Well, Stan, that's probably not unusual behavior for most."

"She even puzzled me more when Lawrence died. She made arrangements immediately to be in North Dakota for the funeral. Strange she could see him in a casket but not alive on his death bed."

Glyn poured us a second glass of wine as we turned to the menu.

Gert

"Cream and sugar with your tea, madam?" I asked holding the porcelain teacup in my hand.

"A few grains of sugar, please," Sandy said with her cherubic smile.

To Louiva's challenge to find something special to make our visits with Sandy more fun, she, Carol, and I arranged an afternoon tea party in the east-wing lounge of Jones-Harrison. The room decor was bright with large windows overlooking the garden below. English ivy was painted across cream-colored walls and the final touch in white wicker chairs around a glass table. It was cheerful and feminine.

Louiva's mother, Lucille, happened to be in town and joined us. We made one trip from the cars to the lounge. Lucille carried in a Japanese sandwich box—three tiers, each one filled with sandwiches that she and Louiva had prepared: smoked turkey with blue cheese on rye, proscuitto ham and tomato on whole wheat, and Brie cheese with crabmeat on white. Carol brought the fourth choice, open-faced egg-salad sandwiches sprinkled with dill.

Our table was set with Louiva's family heirloom English tea set, brought by ancestral in-laws to Minnesota in the mid 1850s. Our place settings were elegant with Louiva's fine bone china cups and saucers of primrose pattern. Add to that, my lovely English demitasse spoons and cake forks with gold, rosewood handles. The two delicate gold-rimmed Haviland plates Louiva brought from her china cabinet for the desserts were quite fitting for the lemon and strawberry tarts, the small cakes with raspberry frosting, and the dainty shortbread cookies of ginger and coconut.

"Oh, isn't this lovely," said Sandy. "It is a shame that we don't observe high tea in America. It's such a civil ritual and has an elegant manner about it."

I nodded my head, "I agree. When we were in England, my husband and I had high tea every afternoon. I'll never forget a particular country inn outside of London. We had a car and were exploring the countryside when we came upon this inn situated by a stream in a fairy-book setting. We were served tea on the verandah surrounded by lush green trees and beds of flowers. I really felt like the Queen Mother."

"Several of us from General Mills used to leave early on Friday afternoons to do afternoon tea at my house. The best was high tea in the lobby of the St. Paul Hotel during holiday season. Everyone in hats and gloves."

Lucille nodded her head, "I remember being in the Drake Hotel in Chicago . . . think it was the '40s . . . the upper lobby at four o'clock . . . full of beautifully dressed people. In those days women always wore hats when out shopping, so we were appropriately dressed for high tea. We went back the next day, as it was just special. Seemed like one's conversation was elevated at high tea."

"The hats were part of the dress and elegance," Sandy reflected, "but I never wore a hat with the personal design of these today."

I had hatboxes full of creations I'd fashioned over the years. I had taken a millinery class back in the '40s and had enjoyed designing and selling hats for special orders. The ones I'd brought for us today were a few of my favorites, and I'd remembered to tuck a hand mirror in one of the boxes.

"Oh, I love red hats," said Sandy, as Carol placed a small brimmed hat titling it slightly over her left brow. Sandy held up the mirror, "Too small, I like a wider brim."

"What do you think of this?" We all looked at Louiva's small crowned hat made of pheasant feathers and gave our opinions with "ooh's" and "aah's."

"This is an all-time favorite of mine," I stated as I modeled a wide brimmed hat of deep turquoise with a peacock tail banded around the crown.

"Don't you think this should be my hat for the day? The blue/green plaid material goes with my blue blouse," Carol said as she held up her choice.

"And, I will wear the black velvet with the soft brim," said Sandy. "It's so stylish with its red underlining. Let's see if it can stay on my head, Gert."

"I'm glad no one chose the yellow straw with the daisy band, as I love daisies. How does it look on me?" asked Lucille. "I always had a daisy hat of some kind for the Easter parade in my home town."

"What town was that?" asked Sandy as we turned to our tea and sandwiches.

The afternoon was one of those magical times when one becomes enmeshed in an enchanted spell. We told stories and jokes, engaged in a bit of gossip, shared family histories, and left out of our conversation any reference to Sandy's health or the home. It was like a perfect moment. Sandy gushed with praise and gratitude, seemed as if she couldn't find the right set of words to thank us. We departed knowing we had lifted her spirits and had taken her to another world for at least a short time.

Mary Ann

It was a beautiful July evening. I had to call Sandy earlier and disappoint her by missing our usual Friday night dinner, but told her to hold off on dessert, as I would bring chocolate malts for us. When I arrived, I suggested we spend the evening in the garden patio and told her I had a surprise waiting in the car.

"What, you dressed Hooper in a summer outfit?"

"No, but it is something for Hooper in another way."

"Well, let's be off and enjoy our malts outside."

Surprisingly, no one else was in the patio that night for which in the end I was thankful. As I brought Hooper to the patio through the back entrance I also had on a leash a new dog, Elliott, to introduce to Sandy.

"What have you here? Two dogs. Not yours surely."

"Yes. May seem foolish but Hooper needs a friend."

"Don't think I could take two dogs on my lap driving to the cabin."

"Well, how about getting acquainted with Elliott. I don't think Hooper will be jealous if you hold him, although, he's such a wiggly puppy, he probably won't stay."

"Where's the ball for Hooper? That's what he'll want to do."

"I have it right here. Let me close this back gate first before I take them off their leashes."

This visit had a different twist to it and one that didn't sit well with Sandy, although she held back any harsh words. Hooper retrieved the ball twice, but on the third time, he started nosing around in the bushes at the back wall of the patio. He flushed out a duck that flew away in panic. I put Elliott in Sandy's lap and called Hooper. As I started his way I saw three ducklings walking behind him. I didn't get to him before he quickly turned and had them in his jaws.

I heard Sandy say, "Oh no. Just like a male dog, has to destroy. Thank God they weren't kittens."

Marilyn

Sandy couldn't hold a book for reading anymore so she took to placing the book on the hospital bed table. She'd have the table rolled up snugly to her body in the wheelchair but found that leaning over to read was a strain on her neck muscles. When Sandy, Peggy, and I all mentioned that we wanted to read the newly released novel *Seabiscuit,* Peggy and I read the book, in tandem, to Sandy. We'd leave a marker for the next starting point, but with so many visitors in and out, the story moved along slowly.

We were sitting and reading in the patio one afternoon, when we heard a male voice say, "Good afternoon, ladies. They said you'd been gone from the room for at least an hour, and I suspected that I'd find you in the sunshine."

"Oh, come join us, Paul," said Sandy, her speech a bit slow.

"I have an ice cream bar for you Sandy. I stopped at a

quick stop just down the street. Sorry, Marilyn I just have one."

"That's okay, come sit down. It's good to see you again."

Sandy motioned her hand to the bar, "You'll have to eat it."

I explained that eating had become more labored and probably the coating was more difficult to swallow.

"Well then, I'll have to find something else for you."

Paul had been a company vice president and worked with Sandy after retirement. They got to know each other as he helped in the volunteer office under her direction. His visits to Jones-Harrison often seemed to coincide with mine and, so at first-hand, I came to admire his display of thoughtfulness and compassion. Sandy had mentioned it was a side of him that was more evident after the executive position.

When Paul left, I asked, "Do you put Paul in a higher male category, Sandy?"

"Why ask?"

"Well, I note that he visits you often, brings a gift in hand, and always finds you wherever you might be in the building."

"Yes, considerate side of him. He was excellent help in the volunteer office, always ready to do what needed to be done." She waited a few seconds, then "I am somewhat surprised he stops by so often."

"Well, does he alter your opinion of men?"

"No, we'll just add him to the small group of males that rise above the masses."

"Oh, you're terrible, Sandy."

She closed her eyes and I finished the ice cream, somewhat soft by now.

Ann

Stan accompanied us on the third clinic visit in late August. I was glad he was there. A lot was discussed, and we posed detailed questions for clarification. We both doubted that Sandy either had the energy or interest to grasp everything of the three-hour consultation. I kept notes and instructions for later reference.

The medical team verified what Stan already surmised about Sandy's loss of body strength, and they were even more conscientious in wanting to provide for her physical comfort. A brace for her head and neck would be delivered to ease the strain on the back muscles, and the social worker would work through the ALS Chapter to get a headset for the telephone and a small mike to amplify her voice. Stan reported she was falling short in the amount of liquids she drank. The nursing staff had mentioned this several times to him. Dr. David said it was critical for the kidneys and elimination and repeated that she must drink liquids of any type. Sandy said it wasn't easy. They gave written instructions for extended range-of-motion therapy along with continued hot packs and massage for her back and shoulder muscles. And they suggested it was time to consider a night sleeping mask for oxygen and a feeding tube for nourishment and medication.

"What is entailed in fitting a sleeping mask?" I asked.

"It requires an over-night stay in the hospital where her sleep pattern can be monitored continuously by a technician," explained Dr. David. "Those measurements are necessary to fit a mask specifically for Sandy."

"When would she use the mask?"

"Primarily at night to provide restful sleep and needed oxygen for her body. She'll then be less tired during the daytime."

"Does the mask ever need to be re-calibrated?"

"No, that is why the initial sleep study and measurement is so important. It may take a few nights for the Harrison staff to adjust the Bi-Pap machine. But that is not complicated."

"Will she ever use the same mask during daytime?" asked Stan.

"Probably when her breathing becomes more labored and her body requires more oxygen. At that time, however, you might consider an alternative method, a tracheotomy."

Sandy shook her head back and forth and said "no way" to that procedure. "I don't want to go that far. There'll be no trache, please."

"I know what you've said before and in your document, but I always want you to understand what options you have, just in case."

"Thank you, doctor, but no," she said in a firm whispery voice.

"Can't the sleep study and the tube insertion be done at the same time, so Sandy doesn't have to set up two separate hospital trips?" asked Stan. "Or could the sleep study be done at the home?"

"No, both procedures require specialized equipment that is not portable and medical personnel who do not make house calls. The insertion of a feeding tube is done by a doctor who surgically places the tube into the stomach. As swallowing becomes more of a concern, the tube will enable her body to get the necessary food, liquid, and medication for her physical comfort. Both procedures are not unduly complicated, but they do require specialized personnel and hospital facilities. And, I recommend that you not wait too long. Do it when you still have strength."

"For scheduling, how much lead time is needed?" I inquired.

"Well, we can start the scheduling process with the hospital as soon as Sandy tells us to. It usually can be set up within seven days."

"Does Sandy have to make all the arrangements?" asked Stan.

"No, we'll do that here and interface with the nursing staff at the home. She just needs to tell us when."

"You may have to tell her when, as Sandy can procrastinate about the things she doesn't want to do," replied Stan.

"Well, since we don't see her between her clinic visits, we must rely upon the request coming from Sandy or the home." Dr. David looked at Sandy, "Don't wait too long."

I looked at Stan, my eyes messaging that we'd better start soon.

Sandy

I think they wanted me to give the go-ahead right then, but I was too adverse to artificial measures. Both Stan and Ann supported the mask and tube but were aware of my apprehension in being away from familiar caretakers and were sympathetic that the procedures could not be done at the home. So I left with those decisions hanging. Clinic visits were scheduled three months apart, and I noted that Ann asked what we should do if I was unable to physically get to the next one scheduled for mid-December. "Just call us," said the receptionist. Think we intuitively knew December might be a doubtful month for me.

Later, Ann remarked about my eyes. "Sandy, what's going on with you, your eyes are blank. I've never seen them without a glint of light."

"Oh, they are?"

"Yes, are you weary, scared, ambivalent?"

"Guess, I'd say lethargic. Not much interest in what's going on. Just want to go to bed and sleep away." I felt tears welling up.

"Yes, I suppose so, but I think you should decide quickly on getting both procedures done. Your comfort is utmost, Sandy. I've given the nursing staff all the notes, and they are ready to help with the arrangements. Now let's call Barb as we promised her. With her medical experience she would be the right one to manage these hospital trips for you. Okay?"

"Yeah, if you say so."

When Ann left for Iowa the next day, the process for scheduling both procedures was in action, which proved none too soon as my breathing seemed to be deteriorating rapidly each day. I am exhausted from the effort to breathe.

My energy for life is weakening. When did I cease feeding the desire to keep it alive? When? Little by little, starting when I heard the words ALS for the first time. A bit more with the move to the nursing floor; a bit more when I couldn't sing with the church choir; a lot when I lost the strength in my arms, and any remaining desire will diminish when my voice can no longer sound words. I don't really want to live this out. I wish some one would put me to sleep, for good.

Ann

I headed out of Minneapolis towards the Wisconsin border, crossing the Mississippi at Prescott. I wanted the peace and serenity of Lake Pepin where Sandy and I, with friends, drove often in the non-winter months. I stopped along the shores at the junction of the Croix River and the

Mississippi thinking of the many times we sat here in early morning, sharing a thermos of coffee. On the opposite bank was the Mississippi Belle, one of Sandy's favorite restaurants. The group had lunch there in June while they waited for Jan to arrive. It had so pleased her. What a gift Stan had arranged for that weekend.

Further on, past Stockholm where we use to shop in the antique stores, I sat on one of the bluffs overlooking Lake Pepin. The lake stretches for twenty-six miles, its depth formed by the glaciers of centuries ago; thus making Pepin a lake within the Mississippi River. The air was cool, a few sailboats sat quietly on the still water. I felt joy in being in the quietness, the joy of being alive and at one with trees, water, sky. Will I feel something like this oneness with nature when I die?

After Maiden Rock is the road leading to Rustic Trail, an isolated back road winding through pastures, trees, and wild flowers. At one spot, a small pool of water forms from water springing out of a rock wall. I've quenched my thirst many times with the crystal clear water. I walk the road. One never meets another soul. It is a mystical place with sites and spirits that seem to suggest stories of forgotten peoples.

After doing Tai Chi in a green pasture, I sat by the stream and felt a need to write my perspective on death and dying.

> Everyone is going to die, but we don't believe it. We live in fear of that final moment, fear born out of not wanting it to be true, even though evidence abounds that it is true. We seldom include our beliefs about death in our conversations, even at the point of death of friends, family, or public tragedy. Rather we

talk about the sadness, their life achievements, the manner of death or the grieving ones left behind. But, privately, I suspect that our beliefs and speculations of death are as many and varied as we are as individuals.

The lectures and readings of Elizabeth Kubler-Ross and Joseph Campbell had led me to serious internal inquiry about death and dying which in turn led me to accept the inevitable, that one's life, as we know it, is mortal.

From the moment of first breath, as physical energy entered my body, I began the first of all inhalations and exhalations that were to be mine from birth to death. The dying process seems to begin with birth—the first breath leads to the last breath—and I've noted that this is the same for a plant, an animal, an idea, or organization, the same as for a human being. A natural rhythmic cycle of the universe. A question then awaits an answer: Does the cycle repeat itself upon death, as a birthing into a different realm? Does the energy continue in the universe? If so, I am not just a body; I am on-going energy, part of the universal intelligence, an eternal spirit.

When did death, the wonderment of mortality, become a topic worth exploration for me? It was well after my children were adults and living away from home. I was nearing fifty-five. My philosophical searching was first born of curiosity, when my span of life still stretched out many years, the time of death not yet imminent. Then came hope leading me to believe human life after death was indeed going to be a reality; after all, my early religion promised the joys of heaven, an afterlife in paradise. Next came fear, as my good-byes to friends who died became more numerous, and I realized I had not a clue as to the meaning of death.

Being intimate in the final phase of a dear one's life moves me to measure again my own fear of death and dying. I think I've arrived at a realistic acceptance of death, the last breath, but not with the intensity of the dying process itself. My wish is for swiftness, in days rather than weeks and months, without physical pain. However, Sandy gives me inspiration and the grit to accept whatever comes with spirit, courage and dignity.

With silent contemplations, I find I have put my arms and mind around the finiteness of death. My philosophical views have dispelled the fear I once held. I could now make public the rationale on which my acceptance rests.

Life proceeds through a series of birthing and dying experiences. A new beginning follows an ending. Birth is the beginning towards an end; death is the threshold to a beginning. We need to say good-bye to the old to allow space for the new. There is an adage that rings true for me, 'as one chapter closes, the next chapter begins.' Change is inevitable and transformation is a continual process. My role on earth is but a temporary calling, a preparation for a transformation. Death is a transition, but to what remains the unknown, and that unknown seems to breed the fears.

My death has to be the most ultimate experience I shall have. It is the portal to another aspect of being that I can't explain nor understand. How do I prepare myself before death is face to face with me and it becomes a crisis, an emergency, or a tragedy? Kubler-Ross speaks to the unfinished business of one's life and how it plays a heavy factor in facing death. What can unfinished business be? I surmise it has to be amends not addressed, love and forgiveness withheld, charitable words and actions left unsaid and undone for some future date.

The journey is of more consequence than the starting or end point. Foremost is how much love and forgiveness is lived in my life. Death comes not in old age. Death comes in not loving and forgiving. Once we cross the line of knowing what happens to us is also what happens to others, we see from a wider viewpoint. We understand in more open and tolerant beliefs, and we evidence compassion in a larger way. If we accepted death as a natural process of a living planet and that it could happen at any moment, I believe we'd live differently.

The fear of death seems to be a fear out of not knowing how to love one another. I've always thought it would be a blessing to know of my death months ahead, so I could put closure to unspoken words and unfulfilled deeds. But, then I must not wait for that final message; I must live love this very day and every tomorrow. To come to my last breaths with no unfinished business and with loved ones by my side would be the ultimate gift.

I believe one's spirit remains in the deeds left behind in memories and lives forward into the mysteries of the universe. Dignity in death comes from dignity in how one's life was lived. The love you have given and the love you have received cannot be lost. And, so it seems to be.

Note to Sandy

Dear Sandy,

By mid-afternoon on Friday, I was heading down Hwy. 35 along Lake Pepin. Fond memories abounded, and the solitude of the road and scenery was just right for my contemplation—life, friendships, value of present moment, and death the greatest transition of all. Sat in mediation on a bluff overlooking the lake. Stopped at the Stockholm bakery for their homemade cheese bread. Turned off to the Rustic Trail and did some Tai Chi in a meadow surrounded by the woods. Then on to Anderson House in Wabasha in time for a walk along the Mississippi before a couple of martinis and a walleye dinner. Stayed the night and really got into Elizabeth Kubler-Ross's book *The Wheel of Life*.

A bit of guilt lingered with me as I left you on Friday. I guess there wouldn't be a right time. Seems inappropriate to get on with ordinary life when one leaves a friend in need who is not living ordinary activities. I also left with the thoughts of the value of friends—you who nurtured so many relationships into lasting devoted friendships. It is a treat to see your circle of friends and the love and comfort they bring to your presence. We are all blessed by you and vice versa, eh?

From my shelf, I found this quote by Thomas Hughes: *Blessed are they who have the gift of making friends, for it is one of God's best gifts. It involves many things, but above all, the power of going out of one's self and appreciating whatever is noble and loving in another.*

Glad we had the four days. Trust I can return before your clinic visit in December. I'll stay in touch and keep you in my thoughts and prayers till next time.

Much love,

Ann

Sandy

Once I said yes, the arrangements for the sleep study were set up for the first Tuesday in September and for the feeding tube the following week.

My liquids are being thickened so that I can swallow them easier. Strange that your throat can swallow thick liquid easier than those of water consistency. Trouble is I detest the taste of the thickener. A cup of coffee no longer tastes like a cup of Java. I've turned stubborn, ignoring liquids unless someone makes me drink, which my friends do. They keep pushing the straw towards my mouth. I see they can be just as determined as I can. But, they ease up when they see how hard is to swallow.

At the suggestion of the doctors, Ann started and Barb continued encasing my pills in applesauce for ease of swallowing. It worked great. If the nurses forget to do the same, I don't remind them and can ignore the medication. I know that I am being difficult and not dealing with the issues as others would want. Stan has always chided me about my determination, which he alludes to as bull-headed stubbornness.

He really rags me about the folly of my ways. "Once you put your mind to what you do or don't want Sandy, you are a tyrant and unshakable. Trouble is now you are denying yourself the medication and liquid that could ease your discomfort. You are actually choosing to have physical pain by not taking the pain pills. I don't understand your kind of reasoning."

"I don't like taking pills and never have."

"Well that was before, it shouldn't make much difference now. I doubt you have time to get addicted to any medication."

"Don't preach to me anymore." I had to wait for strength, "I'll see what I can do. I don't want to be dopey with drugs."

"Well, the feeding tube is going to solve the issue anyway."

"Well, only if I go through with it." I said as loud as I could.

"Ugh, you are something else my dear Sandy."

Stan

I stopped by on my way out of town. I would be gone for ten days and felt badly that I would not be around as back-up assistance for Barb.

"Sandy, I hate not being here but I really must go. Dad needs to get settled into new digs, then I'm off to New York."

I made her use the microphone. "We have Ann's friend, Patsy, as a back-up. She took care of her mother a long time. I'd feel comfortable with her."

"Sandy, I think it's time to consider private nursing care. What with having the feeding tube to be cleaned and adjusting the Bi-Pap for the sleeping mask, which may happen nightly, having someone by your bedside would lessen your worries."

"Oh, Stan, what an extra expense and they'd be strangers. I don't want that."

"Sandy, but you do want some one at your beck 'n call, and the staff here has too many patients to care for to instantly be with you when you buzz the call button or the beeper on the Bi-Pap goes off at night. And, for God's sake what are you saving your money for? Shouldn't it be for you?"

"I'll think about it and talk with Barb."

"Well, don't let that bull-headed stubbornness get in the way of a good decision, Sandy. You know the weeks ahead are only going to get harder."

"Yeah, I know. Go, go, go. Say hello to your Dad. I'll be here when you get back."

"Take all your pills," I ordered as I left her room.

By now she must feel like she's in a hole. I remember an old saying "when in a hole, stop digging" but she can't make that choice. ALS is burrowing down fast. The light at the top is fading. Wonder when she will finally give up.

Sandy

Birdie, my friend of thirty-six years who I hadn't seen since July walked into my room late that afternoon. She and I had shared an apartment together the first year after my divorce. She was just what I needed back then and again this day. Birdie has an outgoing personality, cheerful, bubbly, with an infectious laugh. She stayed through dinner and a TV show, deflecting my anxiety about the upcoming hospital trip tomorrow.

Barb and I left by van late Tuesday afternoon for the overnight stay in the hospital to do the sleep study. Her presence kept my fear and anxiety in rein. I had to get through admissions including the required routine examination, be fed, and in bed by eight so the hook-up could be done in preparation for the sleep study. It was to start around midnight and continue until morning. Barb's previous medical experiences saved me from disaster, and she ended up with way too much to handle. We later joked about the manicure we had planned for what we thought would be a quiet evening, which was anything but that. Besides being my personal caretaker, she kept all our anxious friends informed.

Barb's E-mail

Scott, my husband, brought Chinese food to the hospital for us as no dinner tray had been ordered for Sandy. I wondered why they thought she'd go without an evening meal. Sandy had ordered her favorite lemon chicken with fried rice, and even though she ate only minuscule portions, she said it was a feast to her taste buds. Two doctors, 4th year residents, interrupted our meal to conduct the routine examination required with a new admission. I could tell Sandy was annoyed as they squeezed, poked, and pushed her body.

No doctor orders had been issued for an air pressure mattress, so I had to mess with that. Then the worse thing came to light, no one knew how to operate the sling to lift Sandy to the bathroom or into bed. Understaffed and under trained seem to be the norm for this visit. It certainly put Sandy in a state of panic, and I could read the fear in her eyes. So I put on hospital attire, placed her in the sling and gave hands-on instructions to the attendants and had her in bed by eight o'clock. I promised her that I would stay until she went to sleep and would be there when she awoke the next morning. Boy, patients do need an advocate on hand, and I was glad to have been there for her. I was also glad that I had insisted on a private room directly across from the nurse's station. Sandy's comfort factor was higher with them only steps away.

Knowing Sandy's vanity, you know she'd have a hair appointment that afternoon. Well, so much for her beauty as they rubbed and scrubbed her scalp to hook up the many thin, colored, coded wires. Glue and goo were meshed in about six places. Because she couldn't hold her head up, they had to continually try alternate placements. Boxes of electronic surveillance devices were hooked to both hands. Then they did a trial run with the unit to give Sandy a sense of what would happen in the middle of the night when the machine was attached to monitor her breathing. I stayed right in her line of sight so I could watch her reactions. At 9:30, a nurse came to do an arterial blood draw—successful after several attempts. Got to hand it to Sandy, she was a trouper.

Finally she was lifted from the chair and put into bed and "Yikes" I had to ask for a quick lesson in maneuvering the electric wheelchair. Tricky, but I got it over against the wall. It was then eleven at night, Sandy was situated with pillows, blanket and bedpan and all procedures reviewed with staff.

Oops, one more glitch. Sandy couldn't reach the controls on the side rails, another issue to resolve. Next came the test of the monitoring function and final preparations for bed-down. I give her a good night kiss, as the lights were turned off. It was almost midnight. What an ordeal.

God, I was glad to hit the pillow, although I wondered if I shouldn't have slept at the hospital. Sandy felt helpless and scared. It would be a wonder if she slept at all. I was back the next morning at seven-thirty, coffee and doughnuts in hand for a morning treat for those in her room.

My second drive in the wheelchair was a bit better, and we got her out of bed for breakfast. A couple of hours later, the doctors gave us the report and instructions for the Bi-

Pap machine. We were ready to call the van and leave by noon. Then there was the transfer of instructions to the nursing staff and getting Sandy back into her bed where she could have a good rest from the 24-hour ordeal. I didn't arrive home until around 5:30. It was a weary experience for both of us, and we have to do it all over again next week with the feeding tube. I can see why she was hesitant in doing the procedures; it is overwhelming for her.

I talked with the clinic a lot as we worked through all the stuff, and they told me that the disease has progressed quite rapidly. They said her diaphragm is pretty much paralyzed. Looks like a signal that we better start treasuring each day we have with her.

Sandy

I'm exhausted and tired of my body being handled by strangers. Never thought of ever having to give up my privacy and modesty to this extent. The things we take for granted. I would have broken down without Barb's presence. Any simple thank-you falls short of the immense gratitude I hold for such a friend, and I have so many. I am humble and wonder why I am worth their devotion. Guess they are God's answer to my request to keep my hand in His.

It was great to feel a bit stronger, the oxygen from the sleeping mask made me more alert and energetic during the day. Even though the machine woke me up several times with its beeping in the night, I did not stay awake long. The doctors had told us that it might take several nights to get the right adjustment for the Bi-Pap, and the nurse had to come and work through each beep, each time.

Stan was in for our standard Friday morning breakfast, and a stream of visitors followed throughout the weekend.

An old neighbor stopped by. It was good to have some time with her, as we had had a falling out almost fifteen years ago. Her brief visit was like putting closure to old business, without mention of our disagreement.

Sunday morning I could usually count on seeing my dear Patty. She showed up around nine and stayed through lunch. Her presence improved my appetite, which always seems to please everyone. "Food gives strength" is their motto, and I know they stay with me through meals to entice me to eat and drink.

Marilyn came in for the afternoon and took me outside in the garden patio for several hours with the flowers, sunshine and fresh air. Marilyn and Peggy were my "book on tape" voices, reading in tandem for me the new novel *Seabiscuit*. I'd nap for short periods but felt her companionship. Just hearing her voice as I drifted in and out of sleep was comforting.

Letter from Sandy

Dear Jan,

Thank you for your letter from Maui. It made me think about old times on the beach. I'm sure that having your private chef for a month was wonderful.

Things are progressing as expected. I now have a breathing machine to help me sleep. Tomorrow I go back to the hospital for a feeding tube. I hope that's the end of the surgery and from there things can just run their course.

Stan and Glyn are in New York this week. Jim has Kolden, so I won't see him this week. He'll be too busy playing with the cat.

Barbie has been doing hospital and clinic runs

with me. She's going with me tomorrow for the surgery. Today, while we were at the clinic, she started talking about a birthday party for me the end of October. I think she was trying to keep my mind off the word "ventilator" that the doctor spoke about while I was vehemently shaking my head "No!"

Marge and her husband, Jim, are here and Marge is writing this for me. She has become my personal secretary. They send their greetings to you. Mary comes September 19th. Give my best to our friends in San Diego.

I love you guys,
Sandy

Sandy

When I could no longer get down to Sunday services, Carol brought her spiritual message, hymns, and communion for everyone up to the third floor. I sang quietly within when Gert and Mary Ann initiated two of my favorites: "A Friend in Jesus" and "Jesus Loves Me." Today, a number of friends from the congregation joined us and stayed on for a good part of the day. They had stories about choir and the hymns selected for services and updates from the Bible classes I so dearly missed. I felt included and excluded simultaneously. Staff at the home often remarked that they'd never witnessed so many visitors in a patient's room and wondered how many friends I had. I told them, "I've never counted them. They've just always been there." All in all, I was in good spirits by the end of Sunday, removing a bit of the dread I harbored about the upcoming surgery to insert the feeding tube into my stomach.

E-mails

Thursday: Sandy had surgery yesterday and had complications. She spent the night in intensive care but is scheduled to go back to Jones-Harrison today. —Larry

Tuesday: Sandy is still in the hospital, looking and sounding much better. She can't return to J-H until the question is resolved of having an LPN or health aid with her during night times to perform suction in case she starts choking. She's been doing better with the Bi-Pap at night. —Larry

Tuesday: Just returned after ten days out of the city. Here's a bit more to add to Larry's email. Sandy looks good. Her color has improved with the breathing assistance, and I believe that they are making the oxygen mix a bit richer at night. She is alert, giving us a good Sandy smile and laugh once in a while. She does her best to join in the conversation, but then with Stan and Barb in the room, there really isn't much opening for someone else to say anything anyway. She did wonder how Kolden got along with Jim. Pretty good, I'd say, although Kolden greeted me coolly and hung back before coming into the house. Such independence.

Friends are checking in with me and are more than willing to read to Sandy or come in pairs so she can listen to their conversation. Food is no longer a big deal. The feeding tube replaces what was previously taken by mouth. Sandy is very apprehensive. The choking issue continues to be a biggie with her and is the main reason for the search to have 24-hour personal care. The continual parade of new aides at the home drives her crazy and feeds her fears. She needs the type of assistance beyond anything we as friends can give. Trust the Care Focus group comes through. Glad to hear you are coming, Mary. Let me know if you need to be met at the airport and a bedroom. Or are you staying with Jeannie? —Stan

Thanks for the offers, Stan. I will be staying with Jeannie and I'll get to her house with airport transportation. And thanks for the update. I could sense Sandy's weakness when I called her earlier this week. This will be a hard trip for me. Am working with the ALS organization in Southern California on the upcoming walk for ALS. Think their plans for the event could be more aggressive. Nonetheless, I am soliciting walkers. —Mary

Sandy

What I thought would be an outpatient procedure turned into an overnight stay. It also meant two round trips in the van. One for a preliminary consultation with the doctor at ten on Tuesday morning and an early morning start at seven on Wednesday in order to be at the hospital where the surgery was scheduled for 9:30. The doctor explained that I would be on a respirator following surgery to assist my breathing. He wanted to be sure that I did not awaken afraid that I was on permanent life support systems.

Barb gave another stellar performance, being point person for my hospital stay. She got things done in the hospital that looked like small miracles. She made sure that there was a lift and sling, Bi-Pap machine, air mattress for my bed and a sleeping cot for her. I wanted her with me constantly. She even brought in food so she wouldn't have to trip to the cafeteria. I admitted I was scared, even more so this time since I'd be under anesthesia for the surgical procedure. Would my breathing be affected? Would the post-surgery staff know how to handle an ALS patient? Could I reach and hold the call button? What if I woke up and couldn't talk? I abhorred the thought of being at the mercy of strangers. I had a premonition that this hospital trip would extract its toll from me.

My wonderful Barb diligently kept in contact with those waiting to hear of the outcome.

Barb's E-mail

At 4:06 P.M. Sandy has just gotten back to her room from ICU, going to try to move her to a private room. Surgery went well. Sandy is okay. Tons of people in and out checking her and equipment. I'm staying the night.

At 9:06 P.M. Sandy back in ICU, throwing up. I'm concerned. Sandy didn't want me to call anyone and begged not to hang on to her. "Get the papers," she whispered, "see that they don't use machines to keep me alive."

At 8:36 A.M., problems all night with mucus. Slept on and off. Sandy is on pure oxygen and receiving nourishment through the tube. We might go home tomorrow, although Sandy is still worried about choking on mucus. This has been rough on her. I can sense she's giving up.

Ann

I sense a turning point has occurred or is about to. Mechanical devices—which she didn't want. Maybe I shouldn't have made a case for the feeding tub—did it really make her days easier or just shorten them. Easier would be nice. Shorter, does that really matter? Constant nursing—which she didn't want. Probably it's the strangers she didn't want. Voice all but gone. Just waiting in fear of chocking. Her spirit may now give up . . . mine would. No quality of life. Bed fast. I wish I could be inside her head. What is it like to be so near to death? It's September, only a year since diagnosis. I know we'll not make the next clinic visit. Do I get to say good-bye in person? Better start thinking about getting up to the city.

Sandy

The overnight stay stretched into a week before I was able to get back to the home, my return dependent upon having twenty-four hour professional care. Barb set that up with her typical efficiency. The necessity of being hooked-up to two apparatus drastically changed my days. Yes, I could breathe easier, and yes, I was nourished and medicated, but I was now dependent on devices and confined to my room. I could tell that my right hand was losing its grip, signaling that my days of operating the wheelchair were coming to an end. And close behind that would be the necessity to wear the oxygen mask day and night. All harbingers of the final event that loomed before me.

It's almost over Sandy. How I wish I could fall asleep and not wake up. What reason to see another day? I'm one hundred percent burden now, but I don't want to be alone. I extracted promises that a familiar face would be with me as the end drew near; please don't fail me.

Stan

What a flurry of activity to get her room reorganized upon returning from the hospital: machines for oxygen and night breathing, oxygen level reader, suction, feeding timer, all of them needing plugs to keep them operative at all times. Then the electricity went out in the entire neighborhood and people were scurrying around to find an extension cord long enough to reach into the hallway where outlets were powered by a generator. We tested the panic button. It was vital for calling someone to operate the suction machine if she started to choke.

The room was busy. Marge and her husband Jim, Barb and I were there to support Sandy, and nurses to get the machine operating and the patient settled into bed. In the midst of this the two aides arrived who would sit twelve-hour shifts. Their key role was to begin immediate suction if Sandy had a choking incident. This was now a true and ever-present possibility and danger. After waiting three hours for their trainer, the aides left, but all three returned before her evening closed down. The microphone was delivered. It was to help her converse with the crowd, but it made horrible screeching noises. More paperwork to get a replacement. Ugly. The whole scenario was like an escapade from an old reel of the Three Stooges, looking somewhat comical and full of antics, but totally exasperating.

Finally at nine o'clock, every thing was in its place, the aide was ready for the night shift and massaged her legs as we watched a TV movie.

Each person on the night crew stopped in to welcome her back. Their greetings rang of true sincerity and brought tears to her eyes, which they gently wiped away.

Sandy

Awaiting sleep. . . grateful for the solace and freedom from distress Barb gave with her presence and care giving. She kept her promise to be with me during the hospitals visits. . . hours and days longer than expected. She was my security blanket, anticipating my needs and scurrying to meet them. I was scared just to be there. I'd been frantic without her. A simple thank you won't do for her. What could I buy? Maybe give her something of mine. . . a prized piece of jewelry. My diamond ring. Seems fitting, but she'll fret over accepting it . . . Hummmm, how to do it.

Larry

"Sandy, here is the ring from the safe deposit box. Where do you want it?"

It was now harder for her to talk and her voice weakened with each sentence. Her words come in a soft whisper. I waited as she swallowed, which she did often. "She's done so much. Sixteen-hour days in the hospital . . . long and tiring. I doubt I would have made it without her."

"I think we all appreciate what she's done. She deserves a special tribute. Hey, I understand the buyer of the townhouse moved in last week."

"Yes, that was a good decision to fire the first agent."

"She either didn't do much or didn't have clients," I commented. "I'm glad we let her go. The property sold in a week with the new guy. A case for men doing something right?"

"Rare occasion." Pause. "Another piece of luck . . . I sold the car yesterday."

First I'd heard about this. "To who? Bet it's some one from General Mills."

"Yeah, a woman Patty knew . . . she wanted a station wagon." Sandy swallowed, making a face.

"Is it a done deal?"

"It settles this weekend."

I gave her some rest before asking, "Did you get a decent price?"

"Matched my asking."

"That's great. Now all that's left is the Arizona property."

"Yes, but no luck yet."

"I checked eBay and see the chocolate set is still there."

"Reduced the price, but no nibbles."

"Oh, here comes the physical therapist. Time for me to get going anyway. Your voice needs a rest. I'll stop by Saturday morning, in case you need my help with the car deal. Do you have laundry to be done?"

"No, Stan took it yesterday."

"I swear you must give laundry to everyone, just to be sure they'll come back soon. What a schemer!"

"If you say so, Larry. See you in a couple of days . . .

"Just another ploy to keep your friends around," I chuckled as I patted her shoulder. "You're pretty cagey."

Hard to see her just a shadow of herself. That "get up and go" spirit is gone. God, how will we converse when the voice is gone?

Barb

I knew something important was to be said, 'cause Sandy asked for the microphone. Then she handed me a small package. "For you."

"Oh, Sandy, I can't take this," I said as my eyes saw the ring inside the box. A cluster of diamonds set in a silver mounting.

"Yes, you must," whispered Sandy.

"This should be with your family. It's so large and beautiful. Isn't it your engagement ring?"

"No, I got it after my divorce. Please, I want you to have it . . . my thanks for what you've done. You're an angel." She waited for the emotions to ebb, "It was like having my hand in God's." Her voice faded away.

"I was only doing what I'd promised you. I was not going to leave you alone, not for a moment. Oh, Sandy," and I started to cry.

The emotion of the past weeks and this moment overwhelmed both of us. Where we had held off tears before, they now flowed. I think we were draining ourselves of the stress of the hospital, the fears of surgery, and the hopelessness of the situation. Within me also were the emotions from a mother fighting cancer for the second time and a father with heart symptoms. Looking forward, I knew my time for Sandy was limited. My parents needed me now.

"Barb, I'll miss you but family comes first. Fortunate they have you."

"I may not be able to stop by as often but you aren't rid of me, I'll be calling in."

"Good . . . I'll be waiting. Give your mom and dad my best."

I opened the box again and told her, "I'll treasure your gift. I do feel awkward in leaving with your diamond."

"Please don't be. I'm thrilled to have found the perfect person for it. You are a bright diamond yourself."

I could see talking was harder. "I'd better get on my way or we'll be crying again."

"Call and visit when you can. Love and a heap of thanks."

"Curiosity question," I said as I turned towards her. "Who knew about this guy who gave you this diamond? Was it a serious affair?"

"Never mind. Only a very few know the answer to that question."

"I presume I will not hear the story, eh?"

"Right. It was long ago. I barely remember what he looked like."

"You always have a surprise. Guess that comes from keeping a secret life."

"Shush, be gone with you. Call soon."

Ann Wade

Marilyn

Before the end of each visit, I always asked Sandy if she had any errands or shopping to be done. This day she had a request and with a voice stronger than usual, "Would you mind finding me some small gift bags?"

"Like what do you have in mind?"

"Small, pretty looking bags. Designs or plain . . . get bright colors."

"The ones with handles or those that you fold over to seal?"

"Either one."

"What are you planning to give away in them? That would give me an idea of the size."

"I want to give my costume jewelry to the aides who've been here daily with me. I have a couple of bracelets, earrings, and two pendants that are nice but not gem stones."

"That's not much costume jewelry."

"I had more but these were the only good pieces. The rest of the stuff went to Goodwill when we cleared out the house."

"Aren't a couple of your aides men? You don't have jewelry for them, do you?"

"I know, but they could give the jewelry to a wife or girlfriend, couldn't they? Except for Charles. His family is still in his homeland. I'll just have to present it in the right way."

"It's a nice idea and thoughtful of you. Bet I can find the bags at Walgreen's or Target, can't be expensive at either place. How many?"

"Um, maybe six. Bring a packet of tissue paper also, we can wrap the jewelry in it."

"Oh, I have some at home I can bring. You won't need that much for just six gifts."

"Be sure it's not used from old presents," she grinned.

"This blonde isn't that chintzy, Sandy." And we laughed as we remembered how often we had bantered about my frugal nature.

It was good to see her in a spirited mood. Hope the upswing lasts. It's so much better for her when she can carry on conversation. Many say there's always an improvement before the final fall. Knowing Sandy, she'll make the most of it, cause when the downswing comes, I have a feeling, she'll let go this time around. I'm ready to let go of her . . . there's life but this is not living.

Patsy

As I arrived, three other friends were just leaving. On each of my visits, the room was either filling or emptying of people. I asked, "When do you ever rest, lady?"

"I prefer the people, Patsy," replied Sandy. "Time is a comin' for plenty of rest."

"Guess that was a dumb statement on my part, eh?"

"Good to see you. Staying long?"

"For about an hour and a half. I have to be at work by four forty-five."

"Why haven't you really retired after you left Honeywell?"

"Plain and simple, I can't afford to. I'll have to work as long as I can, no matter my age." I didn't tell her that the many years of nursing home and health care for Mom had to be paid off.

"I received a nice letter from our friend, Ann. She included a poem she thought you'd recognize. A writer named Ward or Wood."

"Oh, yes, Nancy Wood, one of our favorite poets. She writes lovely Native American pieces."

"Maybe you've already read it. It's on the desk in her letter. You're welcome to read her letter also. She's thinking she might make it up to the city early November." We were patient as Sandy got that many words said.

"It's always good to see her. I miss not having her close here in the city, wish she'd hadn't moved back to Iowa. She always stimulates my thinking with her philosophy." I found the letter on top of a stack of mail. "How about we read the poem after I massage your legs. I brought lavender oil this time. It's here in this hot towel . . . it will be warm to your legs."

"Ooh, feels good. You do the best massage."

"Bet that's a compliment so I'll come back again, eh?"

We both giggled, as there was truth to that. Thirty minutes later, Sandy seemed well relaxed and napping. She awoke as I gathered my things.

"Read the letter and poem." In fact, we read it twice.

When the Rainbow Door opens, the Twelve Great Paths of the Moon
become visible, each one connected like spokes
to the vast moving hub of the universe.
Each Great Path of the Moon contains the blood of our ancestors,
the scattered corn pollen from which
ideas and animals were born.

When the Rainbow Door opens, I see my strength reflected
in ten million stars, in the long drawn net of the Milky Way,
and in the deep changing face of the sky.

The Twelve Great Paths of the Moon unfold through the darkness
of my mind, pulling me beyond Earth's frail claims
into the richness of my dreams.
Beyond the Rainbow Door lies the affirmation of self,
the death of ignorance, the renewal of peace,
and the connected memory of all living things.

In this hallowed place, life begins anew.
In this hallowed place, I am the continuous breath
of all that has gone before
*and all that follows after.**

Mary

My last visit with Sandy was in September. I knew I had to be there, as my other self told me it was time to say our good-byes; although, we never actually said those words.

With ALS, Sandy became a more private person. She'd always been reluctant to share her innermost thoughts and feelings about herself, and she certainly was not going to talk about death or dying. She put up a shield making others feel that they could not truly broach those topics either. In ignoring the "uglies," visits and conversations remained pleasant and orderly, although a little strained. Knowing Sandy, I'm sure she did not want to be alone with ALS, and she leaned on her friends to make sure she wasn't.

I promised, or was talked into a promise, to write a piece for the memorial service. I'd be off to Minneapolis in a couple of days for what I instinctively knew would be our last time together. Hope she doesn't ask me to read my remembrance. Emotionally I can't do it. Think I'll leave it

*Nancy C. Wood. *Dancing Moon.* Delacorte Press. New York, New York. 1995. p. 77.

in a sealed envelope. Maybe Stan, or Mary Ann or someone else will read it to her and also in my stead at the services. The night before leaving for Minneapolis, I put my words onto paper.

> How do you say farewell to a friend of forty years? I met you through a sorority to which we both belonged, and you became like a sister I never had. We've been so close, even after I moved to New York. You went through the death of my parents five weeks apart and then, I, with your parents six weeks apart. Although, at that time, we were separated by hundreds of miles, we were always there for each other.
>
> Who else would I have ever climbed the Acropolis with, the Great Wall of China or Borobdur? Sail Southeast Asia, Panama Canal, the Amazon River, the great rivers of Europe, or tool around Europe and cruise the Baltic Sea? We even made Egypt and the lost city of the Incas, Machu Picchu! What a wonderful traveling companion! Always ready at the drop of a hat to take off on another adventure! We missed a couple trips on our 'hit' list, like Petra, Israel, and an African Safari; but my dear, we did a lot and enjoyed each and every minute.
>
> Who else would have flown to New York to be with me during surgery when I was so scared? And, I from California when you had back surgery. You have always been a true and loyal friend . . . and some times brutally honest. You told me what you thought whether I wanted to hear it or not. We were truthful with one another and our friendship was stronger because of it.

I will miss you greatly but I have forty years of wonderful memories that I shall always hold dear. I will see the ancient city of stone at Petra and do an African safari and you will be with me in spirit if not body. Rest in peace, dearest Sandy, you will always be with me. I love you.

Sandy

Mary walked in and I knew this was a good-bye neither one of us would be able to handle.

"Hello, dear," Mary said as she reached out to give a hug.

"Gosh, good to see you. How was the flight?" I said in a whisper and a smile. I'd made the effort to be up early and dressed, as I knew she would be distressed to see me otherwise.

"Typical Mary departure, it was a hectic day at work yesterday, and I got to the boarding gate none too soon this morning. I've come right from the airport . . . left my bag down at the desk."

"Who you staying with?"

"Jeannie. She'll be by to pick me up at three o'clock."

"Oh, just in and out."

"That's a biting remark. I thought I'd get unpacked and then come back for dinner and the evening. Wouldn't you like that?"

"I'm sorry. Just want to be with you. Can I order a tray for you?"

"You can't do meals anymore, I see. Is it better this way?"

I nodded my head.

"I'll either eat before I come or bring something with

me. Would you like me to bring ice cream? How about vanilla, your favorite flavor."

I nodded again. "No, can't swallow it."

The weekend was full of people; Mary, Jeannie and her children, Stan and Glyn who stopped by several times, plus a few others who came by to see Mary. The room was a roar with a lot of activity and conversation. Mary is not a soft-spoken person, and everyone else tends to talk louder to be heard. It was a lot of commotion but welcomed over silence. Doubt that Mary and I could have crossed the gap alone. Amazingly, I never saw Mary break from the room for a cigarette.

Mary

I came early this morning, bringing the Sunday paper, coffee and muffin. I read the headlines out loud, not much interest to her. She is now in a deep sleep after exercises and massage from the therapist and is breathing quietly with the aid of the machine. Hard to see Sandy listless and non-engaging. I leaned back in the recliner and let my mind drift.

Our's was a unique friendship. Our lives ran on parallel paths. Except for this one, I hope. It breaks my heart to see you without energy, interest, or speech. Worse to see you trundled like a bale of hay in that lift. It's indecent even though necessary.

There is silence between us; although what is there to say now. You don't want to talk about your condition and you stubbornly will not use the microphone to make speech more audible. I am filled with compassion, but at a loss for words of inspiration or encouragement. Best I can do is just be here. We are aware of each other's presence and I know we take comfort in that. Remember our road trips? Often we drove for miles in silence—we knew each other so well, we didn't need to say a lot. I'm going to miss you immensely.

Later in the afternoon, I told Sandy and her visitors about my plans to participate in the Walk for ALS, an annual event nationwide. Sandy's friends would be walking in Minneapolis and I in southern California. I'd made contact online with the person organizing volunteers, and I was gathering people to walk with me for Sandy on October 18th. In her soft voice, Sandy whispered the question, "Will it be all women?" We chuckled; even at this late date, she was not inclined to forgo her bias about men. The residue from what had been a cruel and bitter divorce for her.

Our good-bye on Monday was painful. I was wearing the Australian opal pendant she had given me, and her smile told me that she was pleased. Her right hand was in mine and she gave the tightest squeeze she could. "It's beautiful." I reached to stroke her brow and say, "I love you." And, she formed the words, "Me too," followed with "Thanks."

Sorrow overwhelmed me. I was choking and twisted with pain inside. It was a terrible, tearful journey back to California.

Stan

I hooked up the microphone. I wouldn't talk with her without it. She typically grumbled about using the device, but not today, a clue that she had something important to say.

"Stan, I'm not going back home to the cemetery where mother and dad are." A pause. "Once, I had a strong desire to be next to my brother. . . I adored him, but my life has been in Minneapolis."

"What do you have in mind?"

"Lakewood here in the city. Would you?" Sandy had to struggle to say these many words. Her voice was a whisper, but the microphone gave it clarity.

"You want me to work with Larry?"

"No, he said he'd go with what I decided. You know that he's not comfortable with these kind of arrangements."

"You think I am?"

"Probably not, but I'll know you'll do it."

"Always your willing servant."

"Well, if I don't tie this down, I'll be in an urn in someone's closet."

Sandy had never been able to verify if her baby daughter was at Lakewood; although she thought the Swedish hospital used Lakewood in the '40s. One wonders now why those details were kept secret or maybe Sandy never asked. I went right to the task and, within several days, brought back the burial options to Sandy, as I think we all knew her time was diminishing rapidly.

"What does it look like, Stan? Where would the plot be? On a hill? Under a tree? Lake side?"

"Well, there are no places on the side near Lake Calhoun. The available plots are closer to the parkway on the east side. No worry about being close to Minnesota's famous Democrat, Hubert Humphrey." I grinned for her.

"I suppose he has a deluxe site, eh? Minnesota's favorite son." She put her head down and swallowed. We waited. She began again, "Is there a mausoleum? What's it like?"

"Well, you know that everything in Lakewood is first class. The one I saw, still having several chambers available was green marble."

"Wish I could see the locations."

"I could go back and take pictures."

"Would you?"

"You know, Sandy, that Glyn and I would always drive back to North Dakota if you wanted to be with family. Your nieces and nephew would no doubt do likewise."

"No, I want to stay here. Do you suppose there are old records of the babies?

"Maybe. I can investigate. The office personnel might be able to help me. Who do I ask for? You've never told us the baby's name, and I always have wondered why not."

"Too private, but now you can inquire of Emily."

It took six trips to Lakewood to get all the information we wanted. I finally made a small structure of the green marble room and had pictures of the available sites for alternatives. I set up the model. Sandy liked what she saw; a beautiful green marble room in the mausoleum, one wall a stained glass window with a message of "I come to the garden alone." Those words shine brightly from the light coming in during the day and are illuminated with an inside light at night. And the records at Lakewood came close to being fairly certain that Emily was in a plot set aside for babies.

Her deciding words were, "I'd like the drawer in the top corner. I will rest peacefully there." She blinked back the tears, "Now at last, the final decisions have been made."

I reached for her hand, "What a journey it's been." After moments of silence I told her, "You'll have to tell Larry so he knows this was your decision. Besides he has to write the check which Lakewood needs within the next couple of days."

"Can't you do that for me?"

"I'd prefer not to Sandy. Your family needs to hear it

from you that you've chosen other than North Dakota. And this alters the plans you laid out earlier with Larry."

"If you say so, Stan." Her typical reply when she knows I won't budge. "Would you call Larry to stop by tomorrow?"

Barb

We were back to the hospital in the third week of the month. The skin around the feeding tube was looking questionable and the staff thought it best that the doctor inspect it. Since Sandy could no longer use the wheel chair, we went off to the appointment in an ambulance. Antibiotics were prescribed for the infection, which thankfully was minor. Best of all, she did not have to leave the ambulance; the doctor did the exam on wheels. I suspect the aides had not been cleaning the tube properly. I was a bit harsh when I spoke to the nursing staff about it when we returned to the home.

Sandy

My conversations were becoming one-sided as I minimized my talking. It's pleasant when two friends are here at the same time, as I can eavesdrop on their conversation and partake through a smile or a whispered remark of few words. Patsy, Marilyn, and Patty read newspapers or short stories to me. At night, television is my pastime with the aides.

I miss Barb. Her sick parents need her as much as I did, and she has a terrible cold lingering on and on which raises concern about bringing germs to my room. No doubt she is run down from all the extra hours and attention she expended for my general well being. She did sixteen-hours days when I was in the hospital: all the interfacing with the clinic and nursing staff at the Home, arranging for round-the-clock aides and defining what the staff would do (like basic care needs—bath, hair, teeth, feeding) and what the aides would do (primarily suctioning mucus and answering my call button). She stayed on top of getting the right air mattress, which was finally switched to a pressure mattress as I stayed longer hours in bed. Then there was all the paperwork and exchanges for the microphone, head rests, and even a portable suction machine so I could have a few hours outside my room. She continually thought of my needs and managed others so that those needs could be met. At the same time, she and Stan were the communication link to my friends, keeping them updated on my condition through e-mails and telephone calls.

Stan has been my arbitrator at the conferences with the Jones-Harrison staff. We typically met once a month, but due to the recent hospitalizations a review was required, as if my case was a new one. I guess they need to determine if any changes in care are needed. I had very little voice to talk much or long, and I was confident that Stan could proxy for me. He's attended all previous conferences, and Barb kept him well informed of the hospital outcomes. The meeting took place in my room around my bed with a nurse, dietitian, social worker, speech therapist, representative from CareFocus and Stan. There were several issues to be resolved.

The first was the gray lines of who was responsible for what between the aides from CareFocus and the staff of Jones-Harrison. All of it got well defined when both sides finally grasped the issues. Stan did not mince any words in helping them do so; tact and diplomacy was not his style this time. Maybe some of my complaints were personality issues or cultural differences, but I was not in a position to re-train or repeatedly instruct on a daily basis. Stan led them to an agreeable solution, and I had attentive nursing care thereafter.

Another issue arose with Stan's discovery that I had not been on the BiPap machine at night for most of the previous week, the outcome being I was then tired during the day. I have to admit I led him to believe that the night nurse was at fault, but I got caught in the web of that fib. In the end, I had to own up that it was my request not to utilize the BiPap; my complaint being that it bothered my sleep. Even though Stan and the nurse stressed that the BiPap helped to supply lung capacity for breathing evenly, they didn't battle with me. I said no and Stan just shook his head. I know his look and head shaking were to remind me about my stubbornness and that I do myself in at times. But, they let it remain my choice.

Then I told them, "I don't like taking the morphine."

"Sandy, the morphine helps to relieve the pain," Stan scolded.

"I don't have any pain."

"That's right, Sandy, because the morphine is relieving you of the muscle pain you complain so often about," Stan said, looking at me with the 'here we go again with the pill bit' look.

"It makes me woozy. You know I don't like pills. Besides, I saw animals once with too much morphine."

"If it was a cat, that should've pleased you," he said with a grin and then became serious again. "Sandy, you know that not a thirty-minute time frame goes by without you commenting about your legs hurting and wanting them massaged. Why can't you let yourself be helped with medication?"

"Sandy, how about a lower dosage and let us work to

find the right level, for both day and night times, at least to minimize your pain," suggested the nurse.

I finally gave in, "Okay, but I reserve the right to stop."

The most disagreeable suggestion was the one to involve hospice in my care. I'm going to be stubborn and say no. Now that aides are here all day and night, it seems my number of visitors are fewer. If hospice starts, it won't be the familiar faces I wanted with me to the end. And, it's not far away.

The conference is boring and tiring. I've lost interest in fussing about this and that. I just want to sleep when tired and have enjoyable company when awake. All the rest is to no avail. Stan didn't quibble about the things I turned down. I know he has my best interest at heart, and he still respects which battles to take on with me. What a dear, dear friend.

E-mail

We had to have a new-care conference this afternoon, a procedure that is followed after every hospital visit or change in care. I think everyone got a clearer understanding of the cooperation needed between the home and the care agency to better serve Sandy's needs and interest.

The largest issue is the use of morphine for her comfort. Sandy, even with a weakened voice, still makes decisions, like requesting not to use the BiPap machine at night, refusing to take morphine and other medication, and not wearing the microphone. I put it on her today when I entered the room and told her I'd leave if she didn't use it. The caregiver laughed and commented about how I was the only one who could make her use the mike.

Her liquid food has changed. She was getting too full, so they changed to a higher calorie count in smaller quantities. A new communication device is coming this week to help her as she still gets questions from the staff that need her response. We thought it time to call hospice and inquire of their services. Jones-Harrison will set up a meeting with them for Larry and myself. Anyone else who wants to attend, please do so.

The staff is going to work on getting a portable suction machine so she'll be able to go outside her room. I think that would lift her spirits.

The meeting lasted about an hour. Sandy stayed in bed, which is now common practice, until late afternoon when she's moved to a chair and awaits evening visitors. Due to a variety of situations, visitor flow has slowed. Two-way conversation is not possible now; she makes an effort with facial expressions, a smile, and a weak word or two. I see her frustrations in not being able to put her thoughts into speech, as her mind is completely sound and alert. She does like being read to and having company to watch evening television. Patty reads the newspaper to her when she can be here. Patty's health is not up to par and her absence is a sad void to their long-time, close relationship.

I visited the beauty salon downstairs and made arrangements to have her hair done in her room. You know how vain she is about her appearance, and I hope a hair-do might be an emotional pick-up.

I'm sure all the news of the day was another moment of reality for her to accept. Sandy remains such a strong trouper. While she fusses and refuses at times, the wonder of the meds do help her deal with all that is happening to her body and surroundings. They are a blessing although she would say otherwise. That's our dear Sandy.

She still puts on a smile when a visitor arrives—comforting to see the response. —Stan

Larry

When Stan and I told her of our discussion with hospice and said their services included bedside visits, massages, music, and readings, her eyes hardened and she said "No." There was no changing her mind. I knew she'd be thinking about redundant services and costs to the round-the-clock care. But her real concern was voiced when she whispered, "If they are here, my friends won't be. I don't want strangers."

Sandy

The early morning shift on Friday was a no-show, and an S.O.S went out to Barb who drove in from the suburbs to be with me. She is a Florence Nightingale: she bathed me, changed my linens, washed the mattress, brushed my teeth, combed my hair and tidied the room. Her personal care made such a difference. Stan came at noon to relieve Barb. What would one do without these people?

On Sunday, I finally got out of my room for a brief time. Stan arranged church services for me in the lounge on my floor. Pastor Carol shared the church communion service with anyone who wanted to attend. They sang hymns, said prayers and we held hands. It was the best food for my soul and spirit.

Mary

I sent Sandy pictures, newspaper clippings, and the results of the walk-a-thon for ALS, well into thousands of dollars. The Sandy Strutters contributed $1,200 and their time to walk the five miles. I'd gotten red hats embossed with white letters for each of Sandy's walkers and sent one to Sandy—great timing for her birthday.

Glyn

The ALS walkathon in Minneapolis was also a success. Our Sandy group included quite a few church members, Mary Ann and her two dogs Hooper and Elliot, Stan and myself. I work in the non-profit segment of my employer and was pleased when they contributed $2,500 to the ALS society. I think it was due to one of the managers on the committee who had two reasons to vote for a large donation. His stepmother had had ALS, and his sister was a member of Sandy's church and knew of her. When I mentioned the name to Sandy, she acknowledged with a nod.

While Sandy never boasted of her own community work, we knew that she was pleased with the efforts her friends had made for the ALS walkathon. Her cherubic smile and simple 'how nice' said it all. We re-arranged one side of her room to display Mary's hat, the Minneapolis T-shirt and the photos we took. It was a nice showpiece for her visitors.

Amy and Vicki

We played our last game of cribbage. Sandy could sit in the wheelchair for about an hour. Since her hands could not grasp the cards anymore, we bought a wooden slotted holder for her to use. She might whisper first, second, third, or fourth to indicate the card to play or, if talking was too difficult, she'd nod when we placed our fingers on the right card. She played the entire game and won this last one. Her final words to us were in a soft voice, "You are my angels."

Sandy

I've always loved birthdays, mine and everyone else's. By the time I scheduled all of my birthday invites from friends in the old days, my celebration stretched out for a week before and after October 27, my real birth date. Last year, the group from General Mills made it a five-day affair, some one coming by each day with a treat. This year it's whittled down to three days with loving touches from so many. It began with flowers and a song from Stan and Glyn on Friday before Glyn was off to the east coast for business. They'd be back on Monday.

Barb says that eighty invitations went out for Sunday coffee and cake in the private dining room. Probably my last big effort.

Barb

I thought Sandy would be strong enough to enjoy a birthday open house, now I'm not so sure. Those hospital visits really zapped her. Not sure how long she'll be able to hold up. Maybe I was stupid for urging her to do this . . . but thought it would give her something to look forward to. Oh well, suppose it can't do that much harm . . . taking a few hours away doesn't really matter at this point. I can feel death near. Think Sandy does too. Better check with the beautician, she wants her hair done on Saturday.

Karen

"Is Sandy awake?" I asked Marge who answered the phone.

"Yes, want me to put you on speaker phone?"

"Would you please?" I waited until I heard Marge say, "Okay, go ahead."

"Sandy, this is Karen. We have heavy snow falling right now in the Dakotas. Myra and I decided it's not safe for us to drive."

Marge said, "She's listening with a bit of a frown. How bad is the storm?"

"It's just started a couple of hours ago, but the prediction is for blizzard conditions. It's worse north of here."

"Did you hear that, Sandy?" Marge asked Sandy. "She's nodding yes and saying too bad."

"We talked with Larry. I know he'll be at your party, wish we were too. Enjoy the day. We'll be thinking of you. Love you so much, Aunt Sandy."

Sandy

I was still in bed when Charles, one of my favorite aides, walked in.

"Ready to get dressed for your party, Miss Sandy?" I smiled and gave a slight nod.

Charles looked in the closet, "Only see black skirts . . . here's a flowered one. Nice and bright." I scrunched my face.

He scowled back, "Black then." He showed me a number of blouses and waited for a nod. We chose a rose-colored ribbon one.

"Let's put your skirt on while in bed. Be easier to slide it on." He had to work around the urine bag.

Charles rang for another aide to help with the lift to move me into the wheel chair. She helped with putting on my bra and the top; it took both of them to hold me upright and work my lifeless arms through the sleeves.

"Pretty color, Miss Sandy."

"Scarf . . . to cover brace." I moved my head and eyes towards the dresser. Charles found the right drawer and held the scarves up one by one, until I smiled at a lavender and white flowered silk.

"Now, have to have jewelry, Miss Sandy." He brought out the boxes. I let him make the selection. After he clasped a silver necklace and placed earrings in my ears, he said, "You look ready for a birthday party." I wiggled my right hand. He gave a quizzical look and then got it, "A bracelet, eh?"

He finished with putting on black hose and slippers, stepping back to survey me and told me I looked pretty. I smiled and thanked him for the lie. He grinned and turned me towards the mirror on the door. "See for yourself."

Larry took me down to the dining room where people were gathering. Barb later told me seventy-two people had attended. Many I'd not seen for a couple of years. It was emotional, sentimental, and heart-warming as they gave me their greetings and warm touches. My voice is very, very weak and I could mouth only a few words, but I heard their words and songs and could give thanks with the best smile I could mustard. My stamina did not hold out and, for once, I was the party-pooper. *This was it. Going to let go all the way.*

Stan

Glyn and I arrived back in Minneapolis mid-afternoon Monday and went directly to Sandy's. It was her actual birth date, but I wasn't quite sure how we'd celebrate. I was surprised to meet a cousin, Ruth, I'd not heard mentioned before. She drove up from Missouri just for the day. Ruth told us they'd been childhood playmates and had heard about Sandy's plight from Karen just a few weeks ago. Big Jim stopped in later. We turned the evening into a social one, ordering pizza and included the night aide in the Italian feast. Four more women friends dropped by and the evening turned into a small party with a lot of conversation.

Sandy drifted in and out of short naps. I could tell from her expression she was glad for our entertainment.

"I found my book of cat stories and it has the Cat Psalm I thought would be fitting for Sandy and us cat lovers. Would you like to hear it?" I asked the group.

"Of course," came a unanimous reply.

"Sandy seems to be alert," Glyn noticed, "so sit close to her Stan."

"Okay." I snuggled my chair up to the bed and told Sandy I was going to read the Cat Psalm titled One Life Is Not Enough. She gave me a quizzical look.

I have nine lives. Some of these may be spent already, but I do not keep count. I live as though all nine are still owed me. I will outlive my vets and the neighbor's dogs. I could do without shots and pills and the pokes and prods of the vet. But sometimes there is no getting out of it. And I try. Sometimes I don't swallow the pill when they push it in my mouth, but the taste is there and it's a bitter taste. They say I almost got run over. It may be true but I don't remember such things. Even so, I have eight more lives. I will take more chances. Humans say you only go around once. I will go around nine times. Maybe more.

We all noticed the smile when the avoidance of pills was mentioned. Sandy whispered, "Oh you."

Barb

Sandy's smile told me how happy she was to see me by her bedside. She lifted her right fingers indicating a hello, and I took her hand in mine. Her lips shaped a thank you. She moved her eyes and head slightly to the left.

"Is there something you want me to get?" She gave a slight nod indicating yes.

"A nurse?" Her head moved No.

"Is it on your desk?" A nod Yes.

"Oh, it's your mail. You want me to open and read it?"

"Yes."

There were a few notes and a couple more birthday cards. We read those and then she moved her eyes sidewise to the stack of cards on the table. She nodded when I asked if she wanted them read again. She had received over one hundred cards, and I think she had them read to her every day. She'd close her eyes, listen, giving an occasional smile. Patty came in and we took turns reading the rest of the cards.

She suddenly turned quite alert and wanted to tell us something that the two of us could not understand. It turned into a guessing game, and finally, I figured out that she wanted us to know that her right arm was not moving. We continued with guesses until we came to understand she was telling us she could no longer sign her name, and I was to let Larry know he would have to take over. Movement in her right hand was now gone.

I think we all were beginning to realize that the days of getting dressed, of sitting in a chair, leaving the room in a wheel chair were history. The pain medication was beginning to confuse time in her mind. She did not know if it was morning, afternoon or evening. Things seem to be backwards for her, and with yes/no answers to my questions, she indicated she was having difficulty with her sight. When I said "fuzzy" she nodded yes.

Her only word that was somewhat distinguishable was "terrible, terrible." Might be the pain or not being able to talk. I think she has given up. Seeing her in bed unable to move a muscle is tough! What a brave and courageous person. She fought being reduced to a diagnosis all the way.

Admirable characteristics. What a legacy she leaves — through her actions and intentions of these last fourteen months. I'm glad I was able to be with her so often to help in her battle to make the best of each day.

Marilyn

No body movement. I trust the morphine is relieving the muscle pain. The nurse says the morphine and anti-anxiety medication helps to keep her breathing normal. They still give her a higher dose at night. Alertness is waning. I don't think she can distinguish anymore what day of the week it is or what time of day. Things must seem mushy to her. She still gives a smile now and then when she hears a voice. If she says a syllable or two, it's a very soft whisper; my ear needs to be right next to her mouth. Her eyelids still open, and it seems she moves her eyes trying to tell us something. The only movement in her body is the right index finger . . . slightly, more like a twitch. They suction her throat quite often, can't tell if it hurts . . . there's no reaction. We keep music playing and I still read to her . . . birthday cards and letters. I want to believe she hears us. We all touch her, hold her hands, rub her legs, kiss her forehead. We're in a waiting mode. Her life force is very, very weak. Her life has been full; more hours cannot make it better, just more. *Boy, how I'm going to miss this gal, but can't stand to see her this way anymore. Let it be over.*

Larry

I hold the telephone to Sandy's ear. Myra has a last message for her. I can hear her voice; I trust Sandy can.

"Hello Aunt Sandy. It's Myra. I wanted so badly to be there with you but a howling snowstorm made it impossible. I want you to hear once more how much I love you and how much you've meant to me. You've given a lot to all of us. We've had wonderful times, and you have had a great life. You don't have to hold on any longer. It's okay to let go. Lots and lots of love from me. It's Myra, Aunt Sandy."

Mary Ann

I came early Saturday morning, having missed our usual Friday night due to Hooper's obedience class being rescheduled. I relayed to Sandy the antics of the dogs in class. She smiled and opened her eyes briefly. I knew she knew I was there but was not responsive as I told about the three-legged dog in class. I thought she might be taken with the story but not this time. Sandy seemed to have lost touch with us, but as I talked with the nurse her eyes turned towards us as if she was listening.

She became agitated when I said, "I have to leave now." Her lips shaped a voiceless No. I remained with my hand on her arm until she seemed to be asleep. I gave her a kiss on the cheek. I sensed I would not see her again. I whispered into her ear, "I love you." I did not say, "I'll be seeing you."

I quickly left the room. I didn't want her to hear me bawling like a baby.

Patty

Stan was there when I arrived this Sunday; he'd been there for a couple of hours. Sandy was not alert, she was moaning and well dosed with morphine. She didn't respond to my voice, so I just held her hand, stroking it as I felt strong emotions rising in me. The moment was stressful, and I knew, from previous experience, that too much stress would trigger the rheumatoid arthritis, one of my afflictions.

"Stan, I can't stay. I can't stay here with her . . . it's so hard to watch her die. The stress will build to too much."

"I understand Patty. You have to care for your own health. She wouldn't want otherwise."

"Are you going to stay?"

"Yes, and I've placed a few calls, others will be here. We have a plan for someone to be with her until the end."

"Just as she wanted. Please keep me informed."

"I will. Are you okay to drive home?"

"Yes, I think so." I stood and turned for one more glance, "I feel like a traitor leaving her."

"Don't. Please don't Patty. You've been too faithful to feel that way."

I kissed her hand and said, "I love you." I remembered how she told me at the time of my first heart attack, which happened in the bleachers in the Minneapolis dome, "Hang on, help is coming. You'll be okay. I'm not ready to lose you yet." I could not extract such a promise for her today.

E-mail from Stan

Monday: Something happened with Sandy this morning quite suddenly between eight and nine-thirty. Her breathing changed significantly and her color went to a gray/blue, reported Mark, the head nurse. He called and said it could be a very short time left the way she was looking.

By the time I got there her color was better, and she slept very comfortably most of the rest of the day. She was awake for about an hour this afternoon. Monica, the chaplain was with her. She continued to sleep into the evening.

She doesn't want morphine but is so much more restful with it. The anxiety on her face without the drugs is really personally hard to handle for all of us. So this is the status at the close of this day. Who knows what the Lord will bless us with tomorrow?

Ann

I had to miss the birthday weekend, but I was on my way up the first week of November to be with her, as the messages from Minneapolis were not encouraging. I sensed the final days were approaching, which Stan confirmed.

"She is not being as responsive anymore," reported Stan. "She can't move a muscle, sleeps a lot, and is sedated for comfort. I'm not sure how often she is really alert."

"I'm heading out first thing Tuesday morning Stan. I have to stop in Waterloo to see my brother. I have a document that he needs. I should be in at Jones-Harrison by mid-afternoon."

"You might want to call me before you leave Waterloo, just in case things get worse. You know she won't know you are in the room," said Stan.

"Yes, but I want to be with the rest of you attending her bedside, and I'd liked to hold her hand one more time," I replied. "How about I give you my brother's number, you can always leave a message."

I never headed north out of Waterloo, rather I headed home with these thoughts.

Being a witness to love in action was one of my treasured gifts from Sandy's last year. The intensity of looking at death made me more alert, observant, aware of the reverence in true friendship—what one does from their love of another. What did I see in her friends? Devotion in fulfilling her wish not to be alone. They brought grace to her days; gave honor to her being; dignified her life. Compassion in making her days the best possible; in doing so, they added meaning to all the times past. They didn't try to make her perfect, just her days perfect. Guardians of her environment; their visits a benediction—made all our lives richer. Friends verified a life had mattered, had counted. It was LOVE in action. This has to be the stuff that makes for a better world! We ought to keep our eyes on love such as this.

Carol

"Sandy, this is Carol. I'm here with you and so is your God. I'm going to hold your hand and read your favorite Psalm, 139.

> *O Lord, you have searched for me and you know me. You know when I sit and when I rise; you perceive my thoughts from afar. You discern my going out and my lying down; you are familiar with all my ways. Before a word is on my tongue you know it completely, O Lord. You hem me in—behind and before; you have laid your hand upon me. Such knowledge is too wonderful for me, too lofty for me to attain. Where can I go from your spirit? Where can I flee from your presence? If I go up to the heavens, you are there. If I make my bed in the depths, you are there. If I rise on the wings of the dawn, if I settle on the far side of the sea, even there your hand will guide me. Your right hand will hold me fast. I say, surely the darkness will hide me and the light became night around me. Even the darkness will not be dark to you; the night will shine like the day, for darkness is as light to you."*

I felt a slight pressure from her hand. I turned to Larry who was in the recliner. "She seems to be calm."

"Yes, she's been given morphine for comfort. I notice a flicker on her face when people talk and trust that she recognizes in some way that she is not alone. Her friends are here, as she wished. I plan to stay the night," he continued, "and Stan returns early tomorrow morning."

"I'll call Linda and tell her to check in with Stan. She is standing by for tomorrow. Sandy seems to be still and quiet now."

I turned back to Sandy. "Go in peace dear friend. Your life was full of many gifts." I touched her cheek and laid my hand on her shoulder.

* * *

Tuesday at noon, November 4, 2003, friends by her bedside, along with the love of all those who had been there every day for her . . . it was over.

Stan's E-mail

This is the day the Lord has made, let us rejoice and be glad in it . . .

Sandy would be pleased, the bright sunrise this morning was glorious, the crisp air so much a November day in Minnesota. The perfect morning to drink coffee and call a neighbor to tell them the bacon is frying and there are eggs ready to scramble.

Mary Ann met Glyn and I at church last night and created a wonderful display of Sandy memories. It's not just hundreds of pictures but also so much love. Her Bible filled with papers and notes, just as if she'd just laid it down; travel maps, brochures, books, General Mills collectibles, twenty-five year club gifts, crystal cats, cat toys, her walking stick from her last world travel, and the walker that took her on her last adventure in life.

Her picture and beautiful flowers from her nieces and nephew, Jim Ramstad, and General Mills are in place in the sanctuary. I guess we are ready, or rather ready or not, as we have no choice in the matter. My tribute is written and I haven't made it through it yet. Your thoughts, Mary, are on display with the wonderful picture of you and Sandy from days gone by. Two young, energetic, adventuresome women out to see the world. And, oh how well you did that.

So as the eleven o'clock hour arrives in Minneapolis, do think of us as we struggle through this sad and memory filled hour. At three-thirty, when Sandy is placed in her eternal earthly home, "the green marble room, up high, where people can't touch me, where a cat would like to sit and watch the world."

And the blessings of her life to each of us, getting to know each other, and the many memories and lessons will go on to bring us our Sandy moments with a smile in our hearts and maybe even our faces. Hugs to you all on this glorious day . . .

Jan and Mary, here is a grand turn of events you will enjoy hearing. Do you recall the black and white flowing caftan dress that I modeled when we were clearing out the house last December? It had the large geometric design in white and the New York boutique label. Sandy had kept it all the years because she loved the dress, and it was the one she wore when being inaugurated into the state board for ESA. Mary Ann and I planned to hang it on a mannequin next to the picture boards, but when I got a call from Birdie on Wednesday, that plan changed.

Birdie told me the annual meeting of ESA chapters was scheduled for this Saturday. All of them from the Minneapolis chapters were going so she said maybe not so many would be at the memorial services. I told her about the dress and immediately a better idea was born. One of the features of their meeting is a style show covering the years of the ESA. Sandy's dress will be walking down the runway for the 1970's vintage. Mona, her neighbor, friend, and sorority sister will wear the dress. Wonderful—a real Sandy moment. Just what Sandy would enjoy?

* * *

The only reward of virtue is virtue; the only way to have a friend is to be one.

—RALPH WALDO EMERSON

Larry

I got a call from Mary Ann telling me that the choir director would not be able to have a singer for Saturday services; some other event had come up tying up the man who had been scheduled. Could I find a baritone? I told her I would do my best. Who? A lot of telephone calls passed among us; what a scramble in the last few days, too many people trying to find a baritone. I thought of my friend from a local theater where a lot of musicals are produced. Great luck, he was able to engage Dieter, an experienced singer. The church found another at the same time, and we had to delicately work out the final outcome. When it was all said and done, only one singer was available—Dieter. He is really a grand baritone and rendered Aunt Sandy's favorite of "How Great Thou Art" with a stunning rendition. Couldn't help but wonder what accolades Aunt Sandy could have given this male voice, for I know she would have been most pleased.

Patsy

I walked into the church and immediately saw that Sandy was the show of the day. Her friends had carried out her plans in an elegant manner and by their acts dignified her life and death.

As I entered the door, the story of Sandy was displayed

along the left side of the church; personal articles and mementos on tables beneath picture boards chronicled her life. Before stepping along her memory lane, one passed a large crystal glass bowl filled with chocolate kisses by a sign reading: Please Take a 'Kiss' Straight From Sandy's Heart and Savor a Memory!

The first display was a map of North Dakota, a red circle around her town of birth, side-by-side pictures of the child, the farm, the family, and a fabulous beauty pose from her senior year. The title on the second picture board was Love of Church. On the table were her Bible, a candle, the Cat Psalm, a cross, religious bookmark and a quilt made for Sandy by parishioners. Then came Love of Philanthropy with pictures of her many projects, one showing her in a clown suit, including the red wig she wore, and another in a Santa costume she often wore at ESA holiday festivities.

The Love of Travel table was a surprise in that I never knew Sandy had traveled so widely throughout the world. Lots of pictures with Mary, her most constant travel companion, but not her only one. A world map, placed next to her travel folder with documents, highlighted the variety of places where her feet had touched ground.

The Love of Family let us see her parents, grandparents, brother and sister. Graduation picture with her father, 4H pictures with her brother and sister, pictures with her mother in the family garden. After that was the Love of Country table displaying celebration photos with politicians, letters from those for whom she campaigned so diligently, and brochures designed for their campaigns.

There was the Love of Consumer picture board above her 25-year service award, a Wheaties box with Sandy's picture, a yellow stuffed bear she selected for a Cheerio's premium, and the ever renown Betty Crocker cookbook. Next came the Love of Cats, pictures of her darling pets that were her children, so to speak.

The last board was loaded with photos taken of friends who were with her during the ten months at Jones-Harrison. It recorded in pictures the devotion of so many people who had helped her live the end of life in the way she wanted. The board was appropriately titled Love Returned.

Then, in front of the altar on a stand by the urn of ashes was a picture of Sandy in lavender attire, her cane, walker, a picture book titled *The Next Places,* and this reading:

But those who wait
for the Lord, shall renew
their strength, they shall
mount up with
wings of eagles.
They shall run and
not be weary,
they shall walk and not faint.

Patty

Dear Jan & Bart:

I know Stan has been keeping you informed by e-mail but I wanted to add a note. Our good friend, Sandy, is at rest. She battled courageously every step of the way and what a journey it was for her.

She was so happy with your visits, Jan. You and Bart were so very special to her.

Pastor Carol conducted a beautiful memorial service. The church was full, many from General Mills, many from the church, from the Republican Women's Club and ESA. A lot of high-energy women in the room for lunch after services. The other pastor, Robin, read the scripture and a very moving letter from Mary.

Then Stan was on stage. I didn't know what he was going to do, but I knew it would be good. He told me I had to make faces at him so he wouldn't break down. I replied, "Are you kidding? I'm not even going to be looking at you or I'll break down."

He did very well—lightened things up—as only he can. He broke down only a couple of times, very briefly. He came to the podium with two hatboxes in hand, and I knew it was going to be a good show. He slapped one of Sandy's 1950s black hats with a veil on his head and stuck a large black silk handkerchief in his breast pocket. He covered Sandy's life with humor beginning when they first met and became close friends. It was very clever and delivered in a way that only Stan could do. About half way through he said "enough of that" and slapped a bright red hat on and switched the black handkerchief to red, in celebration of Sandy's life. Glyn broke down when Stan placed the red hat on the urn of ashes at the end.

I will treasure the memories of my times with Sandy at your home.

Lots of Love,

Patty

* * *

They that love beyond the world cannot be separated by it. Death cannot kill what never dies.

. . . Nor can spirits ever be divided, that love and live in the same divine principle, the root and record, of their friendship.

. . . Death is but crossing the world as friends do the seas; they live in one another still.

This is the comfort of friends, that though they may be said to die, yet their friendship and society care, in the best sense, ever present because immortal.

—WILLIAM PENN

Eulogy

Thanksgiving for Sandy Weisenburger

Pastor Carol

We are gathered here this morning to give thanks to God for the life of Sandy Weisenburger and all that she meant to us. I don't know about you, but it is very hard for me to give thanks to God at a time like this when my grief is raw. It is difficult to focus on the years of Sandy's full and faithful life, with the fresh memory of her suffering of this last year.

Sandy, a competent, take-charge person of great intelligence and gifts was stricken by ALS, a disease that slowly, but steadily destroyed her ability to be in charge of even her own body. The disease robbed Sandy, the articulate and gifted speaker, of her language and cut off this "other-oriented" person from the world.

We may feel more like yelling at God for taking Sandy away, than giving God praise. We may want to ask God why this happened to Sandy of all people, or why indeed a disease like ALS happens to anyone. And to these questions, we have no answers.

But I do believe that when we suffer, God suffers with us. This is what William Sloane Coffin said as he reaffirmed his faith after the death of his son in an accident, "God's was the first heart to break."

I do believe that God's heart broke as Sandy suffered. I believe that God's loving arms surrounded Sandy as she lay dying, and that God welcomes her into the mystery that lies beyond death. And, I believe that God is present with us on this day as our hearts are breaking. And for this, we can give God our thanks and praise.

Several times this week I heard church members and friends of Sandy say, "If there is anything I can do, let me know." Sadly, there is much that we cannot do, and that grieves us all. Nothing we can do will bring Sandy back to us. We cannot erase the pain and anxiety Sandy suffered. In the last days we would have breathed for her if we could have, but all we could do was be with her and love her, and these were gifts enough.

One of the staff persons at Jones-Harrison told me that they had never witnessed such an outpouring of love for one of their residents as Sandy experienced from her friends and family. I know she was honored by your gifts to her.

And, there is still much we can do. Many of you have been busy preparing for this day, preparing lunch or practicing music that Sandy selected for her service. The funeral coordinators and ushers have readied the sanctuary. Family and friends have attended to many details carrying out her wishes. Some of you have brought pictures of Sandy to share, or have prepared words of remembrance. Some of you have traveled a distance, and all of you have made time in the midst of your busy lives to be with Sandy at her memorial service.

Sandy Weisenburger was a person who loved to give to others and this service of worship with its celebration of faith and love is a gift from her. Any of you who have ever worked with Sandy will not be surprised to know that Sandy planned this memorial service with the help of her friends. She was very intentional about what she wanted to happen this morning as we celebrate the good news of Christ's resurrection for us and for Sandy.

It is a gift to us that Sandy selected Psalm 139, which Robin just read, for our service of thanksgiving for her life. As I reflect on this Psalm, it makes perfect sense to me that this was the passage that spoke to her belief that God cares about us, claims us, and is intimately connected with us. The Psalm portrays God as knowing "when we sit down and when we rise up: verse two." For many such a relationship might not be comfortable, but there is no suggestion here of judgment. The God portrayed in this Psalm is not a tyrant who comes to condemn, but a God who seeks relationship with us. In verse six, we read that God knows us more intimately than we know ourselves, and we hold God with awe and wonder.

God loved Sandy throughout her life from her first cry at birth. She was a faithful follower of Christ and through her prayer life, her study of the Bible, her active participation in the church, and her service to her neighbors in need; Sandy was in relationship with God. One of her gifts to us was her modeling of a life of faith.

This week I was telling one of our members about Sandy's death and she said, "I was thinking of her the other day, because every year she called us to remind us to turn in our pledge card. She always apologized, but we knew and she knew that she was doing what was needed." That is a wonderful description of Sandy. She was a person who did what needed to be done.

Sandy was a giving person. Many of you have received personal gifts from her, and she was generous with her gifts to charity and to the church. An example of giving, in these last few months, was her financing the completion of our prayer room here at our church.

Sandy gave of her time and love. She was a true friend, a trusted co-worker, and a loving family member. Sandy accomplished much in her life, and served others through the church, through PRISM, BeFrienders, through General Mills' volunteers, and through many other organizations for which she worked and gave leadership. I know we'll be hearing more about this in the words of remembrance during the time you are all invited to share your memories of Sandy.

As we reflect on her gifts, we are inspired to be giving persons also.

This week those of us who have loved Sandy are walking through the valley of the shadow of death. We grieve her loss, and we are more aware than ever of our own mortality. But we must not get stuck in the valley of the shadow of death. Life goes on and we honor Sandy both with our tears and with our living. We honor her when we carry on her work of making a difference in the world by helping others and serving God. We honor Sandy with our memories of who she was to us and others. St. John Chrysostom expressed the importance of our holding Sandy in our hearts as he said:

She whom we love and lose
is no longer where she was before.
She is now where ever we are.

If we believe that our lives will not be the same without Sandy Weisenburger, we are probably right. But at the same time, some part of her remains with us. Sandy Weisenburger was a woman who had a zest for living, and she will be part of our lives as memories of her bring both tears and smiles to us in the days and years to come.

God's love in Christ Jesus was with Sandy Weisenburger all of her days and is with her still in the mystery of death that each of us will experience one day. Thanks be to God who gives us life, love, and joy, who comforts us in our sorrow, strengthens us for the journey, and who gives us victory over death. Amen.

Epilogue

Susan Spalding
Executive Director
The ALS Association, Minnesota Chapter

Amyotrophic Lateral Sclerosis or ALS has no remedy, no cure, no preventive measures. Most people have a hard time pronouncing this disease, let alone understanding what it's about and how it affects an individual. Once you begin to know about ALS, you'd wish you'd never heard of it. It's one of the most horrific diseases I've seen. What ALS does to a person's body, how it affects their family and friends can be completely devastating. Yet, it does not destroy the mind or spirit. I've seen this spirit inspire people, who must deal with ALS, to rise above the disease to their higher good. I continue to be inspired myself by the courage and sense of humor and love that people with ALS project to the entire world. It has given me new perspective on my own life, my work, and how I view the world.

There are approximately 30,000 people across the United States living with ALS at any one time. Sandy Wiesenberger was one of about 400 people living with ALS in Minnesota on a daily basis. That may not sound like a very big number for a single state, but, on average each week in Minnesota, two people are diagnosed with ALS and two people succumb to the disease. The numbers never go up and they never go down.

Average life expectancy after diagnosis is two to five years. Sandy's time went much faster. This brings us to another problem that ALS presents; staying ahead of the disease. What one can do today isn't necessarily what one can do tomorrow, and the needs concerning durable medical equipment, communication devices, and personal assistance change daily.

A person with ALS has many questions surrounding the disease and its effects and not always a lot of time to figure the answers out on their own. That's where organizations like The ALS Association can really help. A simple phone call to an ALS Chapter can provide a lot of the help when coping with ALS. There are forty-one chapters across the United States. Each chapter has similar programs, but each is also unique to the state and to the people that it serves. In Minnesota, our local services include: a communication equipment loan program for those who lose their ability to speak; a respite program for full-time caregivers; a durable medical equipment loan pool; support groups throughout the state; patient and family consultation and support; educational resources; a bi-monthly newsletter; visits with ALS specific clinics and advocacy. Our chapter also helps fund nationally directed research. Our staff includes a full-time nurse, social worker and an occupational therapist.

ALS is so difficult to diagnose. The disease affects everyone differently and the patient's own progression and journey is always unique from another. One common thread that I have observed over the years is the out-pouring of love and friendship from people genuinely wanting to help the person with ALS. Some form "Share the Care" groups who give support to family members by helping to take away the daily stresses ALS creates. These groups provide meals, do shopping, take care of outside chores, clean, do laundry, provide assistance with bathing and dressing and giving the main caregiver a chance to get away and relax. They are an absolute necessity as the disease progresses, but people often find it hard to ask others for help—it takes courage and strength. We grow up wanting to be self sufficient and independent, and ALS takes all of that away from the patient and their family. Sometimes people feel they will lose their dignity in asking for and accepting outside help, but receiving all of the services that he/she needs allows the person to die gracefully. Since there is no cure, family and friends can often feel helpless, and a Share the Care group allows them to express their true feelings and fears about ALS. Participating in a Share the Care group is the easiest way for someone to say: "You are important to me. I care about you and I love you." For the person suffering the hardships of ALS, the showering of attention may seem overwhelming, but it allows him/her to know that he/she are not alone and their life still has an impact on the world.

Our programs are all offered free of charge to anyone with ALS in our service area. The ALS Association, Minnesota Chapter receives no federal or state funding. Seventy percent of our funds come through special events such as: Walk to D'Feet ALS; the Blackwood's Blizzard "Never Surrender" Tour (a three day snowmobile ride); the Dinner of Champions; the Luther Eggebrecht Chevrolet ALS Walleye Fishing Tournament; golf tournaments; bowl-a-thons, motorcycle and bike rides. The rest of our funding is obtained through individual and corporate donations and memorials.

We are forever grateful to people like Ann Wade who have taken on the challenge of telling an ALS story and educating the public on the plight of those living and dying with this disease. She is also sharing a portion of the proceeds from this book. Those precious dollars will have an impact on the thousands of people living with ALS today and tomorrow.

For information and assistance for patients, family, volunteers, or contributors, contact the ALS Association:

Minnesota Chapter
333 N. Washington Avenue, Suite 105
Minneapolis, MN 55401
888-672-0484 (toll free)
612-672-0484
www.alsmn.org